Conversations with Kiese Laymon

Literary Conversations Series
Monika Gehlawat
General Editor

Conversations with Kiese Laymon

Edited by Constance Bailey

University Press of Mississippi / Jackson

The University Press of Mississippi is the scholarly publishing agency of
the Mississippi Institutions of Higher Learning: Alcorn State University,
Delta State University, Jackson State University, Mississippi State University,
Mississippi University for Women, Mississippi Valley State University,
University of Mississippi, and University of Southern Mississippi.

www.upress.state.ms.us

The University Press of Mississippi is a member
of the Association of University Presses.

Any discriminatory or derogatory language or hate speech regarding race,
ethnicity, religion, sex, gender, class, national origin, age, or disability
that has been retained or appears in elided form is in no way an endorsement
of the use of such language outside a scholarly context.

Copyright © 2025 by University Press of Mississippi
All rights reserved
Manufactured in the United States of America
∞

Publisher: University Press of Mississippi, Jackson, USA
Authorised GPSR Safety Representative: Easy Access System Europe –
Mustamäe tee 50, 10621 Tallinn, Estonia, *gpsr.requests@easproject.com*

Library of Congress Cataloging-in-Publication Data

Names: Bailey, Constance, 1980– editor
Title: Conversations with Kiese Laymon / edited by Constance Bailey.
Description: Jackson : University Press of Mississippi, [2025] |
  Series: Literary conversations series | Includes bibliographical references and index.
Identifiers: LCCN 2025018519 (print) | LCCN 2025018520 (ebook) |
  ISBN 9781496858115 hardback | ISBN 9781496859044 trade paperback |
  ISBN 9781496859051 epub | ISBN 9781496859068 epub |
  ISBN 9781496859075 pdf | ISBN 9781496859082 pdf
Subjects: LCSH: Laymon, Kiese—Interviews | African American authors—Interviews |
  American literature—21st century—History and criticism | Mississippi—In literature
Classification: LCC PS3612.A959 Z63 2025 (print) | LCC PS3612.A959 (ebook)
LC record available at https://lccn.loc.gov/2025018519
LC ebook record available at https://lccn.loc.gov/2025018520

British Library Cataloging-in-Publication Data available

Books by Kiese Laymon

Long Division. Chicago: Bolden, 2013.
How to Slowly Kill Yourself and Others in America. Chicago: Bolden, 2013.
Heavy: An American Memoir. New York: Scribner, 2018.
How to Slowly Kill Yourself and Others in America. New York: Scribner, 2020.
Long Division. New York: Scribner, 2021.
City Summer, Country Summer. New York: Kokila, 2025.
Good God. Forthcoming, Fall 2026.

Contents

Introduction   ix

Chronology   xv

A Conversation with Kiese Laymon   3
    Roxane Gay / 2013

Hypertext Interview with Kiese Laymon   8
    Sheree Greer / 2015

Heavy Are the Words of Kiese Laymon   13
    Auburn Avenue / 2018

Writing Back to History: A Conversation with Kiese Laymon   17
    Monet Patrice Thomas / 2018

"A Reckoning Is Different Than a Tell-All":
An Interview with Kiese Laymon   24
    Abigail Bereola / 2018

Kiese Laymon: "Absent Fathers and Present Mothers"   31
    Poppy Noor / 2018

"I Don't Want People to Forget the Sentence":
An Interview with Kiese Laymon   34
    Meghan Brown / 2019

The People of Jackson Are Ready:
Chokwe Antar Lumumba in Conversation with Kiese Laymon   45
    Kiese Laymon / 2019

Interview with Scott Peters for the Kenan Institute for
Ethics at Duke University   52
   Scott Peters / 2020

The Flag and the Fury   63
   Radiolab/WNYC Studios / 2020

On Resilience, Tender Rituals, and Responsible Love:
Talking with Kiese Laymon   97
   April Pejic / 2021

"Conjuring Love": A Conversation with Kiese Laymon   103
   Jane Ratcliffe / 2021

Kiese Laymon on Revision as Love and Love as Revision   112
   Jordan Kisner / 2022

Bayou Magazine Interview   124
   Marian Kaufman and Nora Seilheimer / 2023

Sitting in Silence: Special AWP Edition Interview with Kiese   126
   Maurice Carlos Ruffin / 2024

Food for Thought: An Interview with Kiese Laymon   130
   Constance Bailey / 2024

Index   135

Introduction

> ... In you I see the Black folk. As Du Bois thought we might. Now that your inner mirror is clear, I know you see this too. There is a purpose to all this suffering. In fact, as an elder, I can begin to see suffering as a birth. A birth of soul. A growth of it. Now the old hymns and spirituals begin to make sense, though most need liberating from a context they have outgrown.
>
> Thank you for *Heavy*.
>
> —Alice Walker

Long before Alice Walker thanked Kiese Laymon for *Heavy*, his writings, both personal and professional, catapulted him to success. One of the publications that was instrumental in Laymon's early success was *Long Division*. *Long Division* intersects with two areas of my research—Black speculative fiction and coming of age novels—so I was likely predisposed to loving it, but it is also dear to me because it is the reason this collection exists. In addition to the requisite contextual information about Kiese Laymon and the interviews collected here, what follows is a brief reflection on how I came to know Kiese, and consequently, how I came to this project. And yet my story isn't unique. It might be anyone's story because the way that Kiese Laymon creates community and engages with people is a large part of who he is, and this construction of extended family is by design. In the 2013 interview with Roxane Gay featured on *The Nation*'s website, Layman affirms:

> I want my writing to help create a community of writers and workers committed to honesty and brilliance. I want my work to help people work on becoming better at loving themselves, their partners, their communities, their people. I want my writing to help me make a lot of money so I can continue to help out a lot of the poor-as-fuck folks who inspired me. I want to create some of the best paragraphs, chapters, sentences and books in the history of the world. And then I want to go to sleep.

I'm not sure if he's gone to sleep yet, but I believe he has accomplished his other lofty goals through sheer force of will. Or in the spirit of the ancestors, he might be said to have spoken them into existence because words have power. His dedication to his craft and his community is why I'm honored to curate this first collection of interviews focused on his oeuvre.

I first became acquainted with Laymon's work when Jennifer Wilmot, a close friend from grad school, messaged me saying "Yo, C. Bailey, you gotta read this book *Long Division*." Jen was one-third of CMB, our grad-school collective who adopted the moniker as an homage to *New Jack City*'s Cash Money Brothers, and I knew that a member of CMB would never steer me wrong. To this day, I'm not sure what about me said that *Long Division* was a book for me. Maybe it was that I baked sour cream pound cakes and sweet potato pies for friends when I hosted card parties in grad school. Maybe it was my refusal to pay for pecans in grocery stores when I could simply pick them from somebody's yard back home, or maybe I always seemed nostalgic for the kudzu-covered landscape and racism of Natchez that I understood as opposed to the "sweet" tea of racism that the Midwest offered. Maybe Jen heard that I walked up to my friend Shelley when I got to grad school and said, "Hey, I heard you're from Mississippi. I'm from Mississippi too." It could have just been because it was a really dope book, but I like to think that she messaged me because it was a novel by a Black writer from Mississippi, and I reeked of Mississippi. Still do for that matter. Much like the characters in the novel, *Long Division* transported me to another place. I like to think that Jennifer knew that I had brothers who, like City, always carried a brush with them.

Whatever the reason, I'm beholden to her for messaging me because the next day, I purchased the last copy of *Long Division* from Cat Island Coffeehouse in Pass Christian, MS, and like all well-meaning academics, I added *Long Division* to an ever-growing stack of books in my "To Be Read" pile. Months later, when I finally got around to opening it, I couldn't put it down. I was so captivated by the story that I wanted to expose my students to Laymon's work, so I invited him to the University of Southern Mississippi–Gulf Park where I was teaching. Naturally I extended this invitation before I realized that I did not have a budget to accommodate his very modest honorarium request, but in true Kiese Laymon fashion, he said, "That's no problem. We can just set up a Skype conversation or something," and that's what we did! Most of the questions my students had were about the structural aspects of the novel, the inserted sections that Laymon explained were a result of it being published incorrectly. Naturally I was excited to see his vision for the novel come to fruition upon its rerelease. That semester would be the first of many where I would assign something by Laymon, make grandiose plans to invite him to campus, have an inadequate budget, and then arrange a Messenger or Zoom call with my students. It would be another five years before I could bring Laymon to campus through the generosity of various departments at the University of Arkansas, including English and the African and African American Studies program. I was delighted to be able to pay his kindness forward and finally reward him for the free labor he extended on my students' behalf. But I'm far from the only recipient of Laymon's kindness. While I'd love to believe that his charity is expressly reserved for overambitious academics from his home state, I know that it is not. Indeed, Kiese's agent and I often bemoan the fact that he is far too generous with his time. But I suspect that Kiese has been taught, as many Black children have, that to whom much is given, much is required. I only hope that his generosity is paying literal and figurative dividends.

Since receiving Jennifer's text a decade ago, I've had the pleasure of watching Kiese's career grow. In the eleven years since *Long Division* was first published, he has gone from a relatively unknown Black writer to one who has experienced both critical and commercial success. I went from teaching Laymon's works when very few scholars had heard of him to encountering a Kiese Laymon scholar during a Mellon workshop, and I suspect Kenneth Johnson II is only one of many. I went from grappling with how to discuss Laymon's poignant exploration of family and addiction in *Heavy* to seeing scholars like Dr. Rhonda Frederick use "Black Abundance" as a critical framework in *Evidence of Things Not Seen: Fantastical Blackness in Genre Fictions*.[1] These distinctions aside, Laymon has amassed critical success as well. Such honors include the following awards for *Heavy: An American Memoir*—the Andrew Carnegie Medal for Autobiographical Prose, Austen Riggs Erikson Prize for Excellence in Mental Health Media, and it was named one of the 50 Best Memoirs of the Past 50 Years by *The New York Times*. Laymon's self-recorded audiobook of the memoir was named the Audible 2018 Audiobook of the Year. His rerelease of *How to Slowly Kill Yourself and Others* was named a notable book of 2021 by the New York Times Critics, his rerelease of *Long Division* won the 2022 NAACP Image Award for fiction, and in 2022 he received a MacArthur Foundation Grant. But Kiese's success cannot and should not be measured in terms of books sold or awards received. I think he would argue that his greatest successes are those designed to improve people's lives: on his website he actively compiles medical professionals nationwide who avoid anti-Black, fat-phobic biases; he continually uses his public platform to call attention to domestic and international human rights violations; and in 2020 he launched the Catherine Coleman Literary Arts and Justice Initiative in partnership with the Margaret Walker Center at Jackson State University. In the "Food for Thought" interview, he describes the program saying, "the kids learn about the origin of the food they eat while learning about creative writing for a week. And they get a stipend. It's our attempt at love."

I could go on about Kiese Laymon's good works, but I'd rather let his words speak for themselves. Of all my favorite contemporary Mississippi writers, Kiese is one of the most prolific on social media providing commentary on topics ranging from American politics, basketball, foreign policy, hip-hop, up and coming writers, to basketball again. What you'll find in these reflections is the same thing you'll find if you have a conversation with him, read his fiction or prose, or even if you listen to the podcast that he recently launched with fellow writer Deesha Philyaw. In his dissertation chapter "#BIGBOYSARECUTE: *Heavy*, Black Boys' Body Literacy, and Fat Black Men's Desirability," Johnson II writes: "As Laymon bears his soul about the myriad and conflating trauma in his life, his conversations around his fat black body introduces necessary questions about what black men are taught about their bodies, how they understand their space in society, and the opportunities to have vulnerable conversations about those bodies, especially in a society that deems them—especially fat ones—undesirable, Other, and disposable."[2]

Laymon adeptly handles such issues, and many others that are germane to his work, with wit and candor, and the interviews in this collection bear this out. His writing always feels authentic, that elusive quality that many writers, indeed many people, strive for. You'll find that Laymon's voice is consistent across genres and media. For Laymon, the personal is political, so his perspective is always informed by his Southernness, his Blackness, his insecurities, his family. He is not singular in this regard. Kiese Laymon portrays folks who are marred by geography and family as much as they are by racism. He, Jesmyn Ward, and Natasha Tretheway all eloquently render the painful incongruities of life in Mississippi: the beauty, the simplicity, and at times, the brutality. Yet, Laymon's voice is distinctive in the way he strikes a balance between humor and honesty. I like to describe Laymon's musings as relishing in the petty, a distinction that he'd likely embrace and wear like a proverbial badge of honor.

In *Conversations with Kiese Laymon*, you'll find sixteen interviews that cover topics ranging from writing to politics. While I would argue that the interviews here are some of his most personal and provocative ones, Kiese grants a lot of interviews. He also does an excellent job compiling resources, including his interviews, for his followers. Instead, these interviews center home, be that Mississippi or the writing desk. The interviews collected here reflect his complicated relationship with things that he loves: food, family, and his home state. The interviews and even this introduction seek to capture a literary titan's greatness while he's in his prime. Friend and fellow Mississippi writer Addie Citchens says of Laymon: "Kiese just gets it right. He gets the pain, the joy, the funny, the brilliance, the Mississippi—so right. And sometimes I'm terrified at the breadth of the work, but I'm always thankful." I couldn't agree more. It's why so many fellow writers, scholars, students, and general readers inside and outside the state refer to Laymon using the familiar sobriquet "fam," even while we lack any familial connection. It's because in Laymon's public persona and his writings we see something of ourselves. We see our humility; our brilliance; our anger; our humor. We see home. For this reason, I include an interview about Mississippi that Kiese conducted, an anomaly in the Literary Conversations Series, and yet, the interview is essential for understanding Laymon's legacy. It reflects his commitment to our state, but more importantly, to our people. It is with this thought that I invite you to explore the conversations that other critics and creatives have had with one of Mississippi's most celebrated and cherished writers. I invite you to come home to Mississippi with me.

There are many people who I should thank for helping this project come together, but the most obvious is the writer himself for indulging my frequent requests and for answering many questions over the year or so that it took this project to come together. I'm thankful to each and every academic, creative writer, or publisher who granted the University Press of Mississippi reprint permission. This collection would not be possible without their enthusiastic cooperation. Along that same vein, I'm especially grateful to Mary Heath, the acquisitions editor who I harassed at an Annual Folklore Society meeting when she was trying to sell books. I insisted that UPM NEEDED *Conversations with Kiese Laymon* or they couldn't be the University Press of Mississippi. Of course, the press has excellent series for folklorists and African American Studies scholars like me, but the Literary Conversations remains one of my personal favorites, so I'm delighted that Mary gave the project the greenlight. Whether or not she thinks I'm insane remains to be seen! I would like to thank writer and friend Addie Citchens and scholar Kenneth L. Johnson II for humoring me by providing quotes about Kiese Laymon and his writing. Thank you to my colleagues at Georgia

State University in the English and Africana Studies Department. A special thank you goes out to Joanay Tran, a graduate student in the Women, Gender, and Sexuality Studies Institute at Georgia State University. Jo's organizational skills were invaluable as I started to compile interviews. I'm also grateful to Jennie Burnett, and the Institute of Women, Gender, and Sexuality Studies at Georgia State University. Although I am an affiliated faculty member of the institute, I have yet to teach a course for the unit or direct a student thesis. Despite this fact, when I requested the assistance of a graduate student to complete *Conversations with Kiese Laymon*, she immediately said, "No problem." My only hope is that the appointment has been as beneficial for the graduate student as it has been for me. Most importantly, I'd like to thank my family for their unceasing support and patience.

CB

Notes

1. Frederick reads Barbara Neely's character Blanche through the lens of Black abundance in her first chapter, "Fantastically Black Blanche White: Barbara Neely's *Blanche on the Lam*."

2. Kenneth Johnson II, "#BIGBOYSARECUTE: *Heavy*, Black Boys' Body Literacy, and Fat Black Men's Desirability," *Boy Man: Multiple Literacies and Navigating Southern Boyhood in the Works of Kiese Laymon*, PhD diss. (Florida State University, 2021), 4–5.

Chronology

1974	Born August 15, 1974, in Jackson, Mississippi.
1998	BA from Oberlin College.
2001	MFA in Fiction from Indiana University.
2013	*Long Division* published by Bolden (Agate Press).
2013	*How to Slowly Kill Yourself and Others in America* published by Bolden (Agate Press).
2018	*Heavy: An American Memoir* published by Scribner.
2019	*Heavy: An American Memoir* won the Andrew Carnegie Medal for Autobiographical Prose, Barnes and Noble Discovery Award, Austen Riggs Erikson Prize for Excellence in Mental Health Media, named one of the 50 Best Memoirs of the Past 50 Years by *The New York Times*. Laymon's self-recorded audiobook of the novel was named the Audible 2018 Audiobook of the Year.
2020	Started the Catherine Coleman Literary Arts and Justice Initiative, a program based out of the Margaret Walker Center at Jackson State University.
2020–2021	Received the Radcliffe Fellowship at Harvard.
2021	*How to Slowly Kill Yourself and Others* was rereleased by Scribner Press. It was named a notable book of 2021 by the New York Times Critics.
2022	Named the Libbie Shearn Moody Professor of English and Creative Writing at Rice University. Rerelease of *Long Division* won the 2022 NAACP Image Award for fiction. Received MacArthur Foundation Grant.
July 2024	Launches Reckon True Stories podcast with creative writer Deesha Philyaw.
April 2025	*City Summer, Country Summer* children's book published by Kokila.

Conversations with Kiese Laymon

A Conversation with Kiese Laymon

Roxane Gay / 2013

From *The Nation*'s website, September 12, 2013. © 2013 The Nation Company. All rights reserved. Used under license.

I first encountered Kiese Laymon's writing when I read *How to Slowly Kill Yourself and Others in America: A Remembrance*. I was stunned into stillness. For a long while I simply sat with Laymon's words and tried to absorb what he had done. Then I reread the essay and was stunned into stillness again. I'm not going to lie. I was jealous—straight up, green-eyed, how can someone write this damn well, jealous. That passed quickly, though, because Laymon's writing was too important and too necessary for me to be trifling.

Laymon's writing has reminded me that I read to better know the world and how it shapes us. As I've gotten to know Laymon's work through his essays, collected in a book also titled *How to Slowly Kill Yourself and Others in America*, and his debut novel, *Long Division*, I've been better able to appreciate how complex and varied the Black experience in America can be.

His fiction, in particular, thrills me. *Long Division* is an ambitious novel, and though it is raw and flawed, it is the most exciting book I've read all year. There's nothing like it, both in terms of the scope of what the book tackles and the writing's Afro Surrealist energy. There's time travel and a story within the story. From the first page to the last, something bigger than the story is happening.

Long Division is, in its gutsy heart, a novel about how a young Black boy grapples with coming into manhood in the South. I knew I would love this book from the first chapter when Citoyen "City" Coldson is competing against LaVandar Peeler in a "Can You Use That Word in a Sentence" competition. The "Can You Use That Word in a Sentence" contest was started in the spring of 2006 after states in the Deep South, Midwest, and Southwest complained that the Scripps Spelling Bee was geographically biased. The novel is full of such seductively clever bits.

And then City is trying to explain the word "n---a." He explains to his friend MyMy:

"Damn girl. Didn't I just tell you not to say that word? Look. I know that I'm a n---a. I mean . . . I know I'm black . . . but 'n---a' means below human to some folks and it means superhuman to some other folks. Do you even know what I'm saying? And sometimes it means both to the same person at different times. And, I don't know. I think 'n---a' can be like the word 'bad.' You know how 'bad' means a lot of things? And sometimes, 'bad' means 'super good.' Well, sometimes being called a 'n---a' by another person who gets treated like a 'n---a' is one of the top seven or eight feelings in the world. And other times, it's in the top two or three worst feelings. Or, maybe . . . shoot. I don't know. I couldn't even use the word in a sentence, MyMy. Ask Someone else. Shoot. I don't even know."

In one exchange, Laymon captures the fraught nuance of the n-word and its implications in ways that are organic to the fictional world he is creating. The prose consistently offers incisive commentary, intriguing storytelling and so much promise for Laymon's future work. Laymon and I recently talked, via email, about race, his writing and what words can make possible.

Roxanne Gay: Is Blackness a burden? If so, how do we carry it without breaking our backs?

Kiese Laymon: Blackness, in and of itself, isn't a burden at all. In this nation, we all carry the immense burden of being human, but our backs are sore as hell because white Americans have failed to compassionately reckon with the worst of white folks. They tried to destroy us intellectually, psychologically, emotionally, economically, and we helped them out quite a bit. When people with more access to healthy choices and second chances obsessively want, and really need, you to have even less access to healthy choices and second chances, your back and your heart will tend to break. The wonder is that we're not broken. We're not broken. The wonder is that we're still here creating, still willing ourselves into generative kinds of human beings even though we're really, really, really, tired.

RG: You wrote about how your mother raised you never to forget you were born on parole. How are young Black children supposed to thrive under such conditions? Do you try to answer such an impossible question in your writing?

KL: I think you thrive partially through milking your senses and your imagination and placing yourself within a larger community of tough, sensitive workers. My mother conflated survival with joy. She wanted me to be happy if I simply survived. I get it. I really get it. When a nation is implicitly and explicitly intent on destroying you and your son, survival feels like a win. But fuck that. As all-consuming and destructive as white supremacy is, it won't win. When I read your stuff, for example, I see that white supremacy hasn't won. I guess I'm dumb, but I believe in us and I believe that even though the game is rigged, we can actually win with love, tenacity, compassion, community, and the will to fight and strategize when we have to. The alternative is death.

RG: You write both fiction and nonfiction. Which is your first love?

KL: My first love was fiction. My grandma would give me these notebooks she wanted me to take notes in while we were in church and Sunday school. Sometimes I'd write these stories about this hole in the ground across the road from her house. Most of the time, I'd write these stories that ended with the sexy deaconesses in church telling me how sexy I was for an eight-year-old. In eleventh grade, I fell in love with the essay.

RG: There's a real elegance to *Long Division*, particularly in how you balance telling a story with really incisive racial commentary. What did it take to achieve that balance? It takes a devotion to character, place, and Black American literary tradition. And lots and lots of revision. In *Long Division*, the book moves back and forth through time and also is quite coy about genre. I really enjoyed that playfulness and the nod to Afro Surrealism. Why don't we see more of such work from Black writers? Both Afro Futurism and Afro Surrealism seem ripe with opportunity for writers of color.

KL: It's weird that we don't see it in literature. I wanna blame the publishers, but I'm not sure that's fair. I know that we see tons of Afro Surrealism in our music. Tons. Hip-hop, for all the true and dishonest shit that people talk about it, is our most explicit example of Afro Surrealism and Afro Futurism. I mean, my favorite rapper and writer calls himself André 3000. He has works called *ATLiens, Stankonia, Aquemini*. We don't have to look far for popularized versions of Afro Surrealism of Afro Futurism. We just need more writers willing to engage with our best storytellers, whether those storytellers are literary storytellers or not.

RG: Though I enjoyed the book, I struggled with the end of *Long Division*. I wanted the book as a whole to deliver more fully on its immense promise. Were you happy with how *Long Division* turned out?

KL: People who love the book tend to love the last few chapters, while a number of readers I trust, like you, have said that they wanted it to deliver more. I'm not sure that those readers who loved the book "get the ending," but I think they might understand some of what I'm trying to do at the end with metafiction, the idea of runaway characters, the consequences of being young, Black, and Southern in a crazy-making nation filled with crazy-making characters and narratives. The ending literally is asking readers to reread the book and consider all the sentences, consider who's writing whom, consider all that that led these kids underground. At the end, we see the beginnings (maybe) of a community of young Black kids sweating, crying, laughing, wondering, wandering, and creating under the ground in rural Mississippi. Together. It's pretty daring and I'm sure I could get it "closer to right" with a few more revisions.

RG: Why, do you think, publishing, even in 2013, remains so resistant to welcoming new voices to the literary table?

KL: Most mainstream publishers don't understand our work or our communities. But they understand clicks. So I think we're seeing a change in what folks are willing to publish recently because they see that a lot of shit that they don't understand is getting thousands and thousands of clicks. The South figures heavily in both your fiction and nonfiction. What does it mean to represent the South in writing as a Black man? What is the South to you? I try hard as I can to never "represent" the South. I want to explore my South, honor my South, extend the traditions of my South, but I don't want to represent it, translate it, or synthesize it for folks unwilling to love or imagine our people. The South, generally, and Mississippi, specifically, is home. It's home. It's why I read, why I write, why I try to love, and why it's hard as hell to beat me. We have been and can be a model of transformation for the rest of the nation and world. But we gotta stop being so devoted to death and destruction.

RG: Memory seems so critical to your writing. How do you preserve memory?

KL: I preserve memory through writing. I have to write to remember, to reckon with my memories. I write a lot of hours every day because I'm not good enough not to. When I'm not remembering and reckoning, I'm a terrible person.

RG: Who have been some of your influences, and how do you acknowledge those influences in your work?

KL: Jesmyn Ward, Margaret Walker Alexander, Charlie Braxton, André 3000, Octavia Butler, James Baldwin, Eve Dunbar, Toni Cade Bambara, Imani Perry, the Brothers Writing to Live Crew, hip-hop journalism in the 1990s, dream hampton, Hua Hsu, my mother, grandmother, auntie, students, and the part of me that wants to be one of the greatest literary workers ever are the only reasons I'm able to write a decent paragraph every now and then. That's just the truth. I write to these folks in everything I create, and I hope they can see and feel their inspiration in my sentences.

RG: Is it possible for you to write without race in some way shaping what you do?

KL: I think it's possible for me to write without race shaping what I do because "shaping" is primarily a tool of revision, right? But it's impossible for race not to in some way mingle with my prose. That mingling should happen in a way that explores intersections of sexuality, gender, money, and geography. Race and sexuality and gender and class and geography and history are always ingredients in everything ever written. Most writers are too lame to accept this as absolute truth.

RG: I don't think enough writers, and particularly writers of color, talk about ambition. Where do you want your writing to take you?

KL: I want my writing to help create a community of writers and workers committed to honesty and brilliance. I want my work to help people work on becoming better at loving themselves, their partners, their communities, their people. I want my writing to help me make a lot of money so I can continue to help out a lot of the poor-as-fuck folks who inspired me. I want to create some of the best paragraphs, chapters, sentences, and books in the history of the world. And then I want to go to sleep.

RG: What do you like most about your writing?

KL: Structurally, every now and then, I do some things that haven't really been done before, like in *Long Division* and the essay "How to Slowly Kill Yourself and Others in America." I like that sometimes it's really unafraid of the truth. Mostly, I love that the work I've created since July 2012 is going to last long after I'm gone.

Hypertext Interview with Kiese Laymon

Sheree Greer / 2015

From *Hypertext* online, March 31, 2015. Reprinted with permission.

Sheree Greer: "You are the Second Person" was our first date, and I knew before you walked me to my door that I wanted to marry you. I wish I was bullshitting. In that piece, you discuss the very real, extremely frustrating process of trying to get your novel, *Long Division*, published and on the shelves. *Long Division*, an incredibly imaginative and experimental novel that compels you to follow Citoyen "City" Coldson as he traverses the past, the present, and the future through a hole in a small town in Mississippi, was batted around a lot until it found a home at Agate Bolden. Your essay talks about some of your challenges, one in particular being that you wanted your grandma to know you're a "real writer," as the tool of an agent says you have the makings of "a Black writer." What does being a "Black writer" mean to you? And is it important to say it, to claim it?

Kiese Laymon: Being a Black writer means that I have the wonderfully huge responsibility of building on the Black literary traditions before me while writing to the next generation of courageous Black readers and writers. We must claim it. I want everything I write to be honest and in the real and imaginative service of Black folks, particularly Mississippi Black folks.

SG: In an article worthy of the Don Lemon Journalism Award, Ben Okri essentially wrote that Black and African writing is stymied by our subject matter, our work relegated to slave narratives and tales of past and current oppressions. Dude said what Black and African writers produce is "less varied, less enjoyable, and, fatally, less enduring." He cited work from the "literary canon," and switched out myopic for magic in his description of the work found there. When you write, do you think about where or how your work will be situated in the literary landscape? How it will or won't be identified by the publishing and literary world?

KL: Ben Okri was just wrong. He's exposing himself and I want to say that I'm sorry that white folks and white racial supremacy have his work and imagination in a stranglehold. Black storytelling can get him out of that stranglehold. Just not sure he wants out. Being a willful victim of white racial supremacy as a Black artist is lucrative. I don't really think of the literary landscape as much as I think about whether the folks who artistically created me will be excited about the work.

SG: So it's probably obvious at this point that I'm trying too hard. I want you to like me. I want you to think I'm smart. Plus I feel like I got you on the line, so it's like, reading your work and getting a chance to talk to you about it got me all giddy and nervous. I'm being all "motor-mouf" like my mama used to call me for telling my jama what was going on in our house any time she asked me. And now I'm being wack and sensitive and needy.

Let's start over, but you should totally answer those previous questions, and Imma just stop writing a damn thesis before I start each one. Okay. Here we go.

Your essay "My Vassar College Faculty ID Makes Everything OK" calls out the rabid racial profiling, and worse, that takes place on your college campus, and, because a college campus is most times a microcosm of the town, or city, or state that the college campus resides, the piece inevitably calls out the racial profiling that is a matter of course in America. You write this piece without flinching, or at least it reads that way, yet I have to beg the question, did you flinch? Did you, or do you, have Jacob-Gabriel MMA fights with yourself about how honest to be, how open and raw to be on the page?

KL: This is the best interview ever, Sheree. I didn't flinch but I revised it about 102 times. At first, I think I went too hard at the president and dean of my college. Then I realized that though they have been completely negligent, they don't deserve to be at the end of my ink. So I broadened the piece and spoke to us about what we're dealing with and about how we go forward and inward in these sick institutions. I'm a really insecure dude in a lot of ways, but not in this writing thing. I know Vassar College is lucky to have me. They just are. There are few folks on earth doing what I can do with fiction and the essay. That's just true. Jesmyn and Roxane can do things I can't do. But I'm steadily learning and getting better. It's all love. All work.

SG: I caught Jesmyn Ward on NPR, *The Diane Rehm Show* to be exact, "Race Relations and the Search for Justice in Ferguson, Missouri," and she was introduced as exactly what she is, a novelist, among other amazing things, I'm certain. Couple that with Chimamanda Adichie getting the Beyhive buzzing about feminism, plus countless other intersections of politics and fiction, social responsibility and fiction, and I'm reminded of Baldwin, Lorde, Sanchez, and Giovanni, and the tradition of artist-activists. Do you consider yourself an activist? Why or why not?

KL: Great question. I am an activist. And I am an artist whose work has influenced some of the most committed social activists in our country. And yes, I do consider it my responsibility to actively fight for the world I want to see. So yes, writing is part of my activism, but it's not the same as the organizing, strategizing, and executing. I want my work on the page and every other place to do its part to ensure good love, healthy choices, and second chances for our people.

SG: And now my damn questions are too long. Unfortunately, or fortunately, only you can decide that, there ain't nothing to be done about that. So please, bear with me. I do, after all, have you on the line.

On *Left of Black* with Mark Anthony Neal, you talked about the "performative" aspect of your writing, an idea of "changing audiences" within a piece. That sounds like breaking the rules, but you go O-Dog on everything you write; it's like you don't care, but you do care. More than most. But about whom most specifically? Who is your audience?

KL: You are my primary audience. You're right there at the front. I know a lot of people are watching, but they don't get to be in front unless I want them to be. My teachers, my sixteen-year-old self, my little cousin, Baldwin, Lorde, Badu are front and center of everything I write. But I change audiences sometimes in a piece. I think we have to.

SG: You wrote an essay about a $169.75 pair of red Kangs, an essay indicative of your complexity as a writer. How do you do that? Write about a pair of sneakers with a contemplative flair that considers poverty, hopes, dreams, giving back, privilege, and sweatshops? Do you start with an object or experience and just follow it where it goes until you arrive in downtown Brilliant, or is your approach to essay writing more calculated?

KL: You're just being nice. That essay was not good at all. I needed more space and time to do what I wanted to do. It's full of ambition but not so full of precision. I hate when I have to turn something in that's just not dope. That one wasn't dope.

SG: In your novel, *Long Division*, you take on the issue of propriety in a lot of ways: City is always thinking about how people want him to act, how Black people are supposed to act or behave, and balks when watching his grandmother, one of the strongest women he knows, if not the strongest, turn it on for the white folks. How intentional was this theme of propriety? How important was it for City to not only notice the way people act and the way people want him to act, but to basically, at every turn, do whatever the hell he wanted to?

KL: That question is the core of City. How can this young City, this young Citizen, engage in the act of becoming imaginatively human when so many folks are telling him that he's going to be punished for being too Black, for being too free. He's really questioning how the greatest people in his life can also be so afraid. That's really what he's saying over and over again. "Why y'all scared?" By the end (or the beginning) he understands, but his response is not to give folks what they want. He goes back under the ground [to] heal, love, and get ready to come out again.

SG: Roxane Gay called *Long Division* "raw and flawed" while calling it "the most exciting book she's read all year." Do you agree? Is your novel raw? Is it flawed? Is there anything you would change if you could?

KL: Yeah, every novel is flawed. Every piece of art is flawed. I've revised portions of *LD* since it has come out, but I'd hope that every author has done that with their work. There were really important scenes where Black women characters were talking to Black women characters when they didn't know City was listening. Those were important scenes in terms of plot, but also in terms of what I'm trying to explore about race and gender in that book. We need more scenes in books written by Black men where women are talking to women about shit other than Black men. It's crucial. So yeah, in my revisions, scenes with Grandma, Mama Lara, Baize, and Shalaya Crump are back in there. Other than that, I hope folks understand that even though it's written in a voice we rarely consider hyperliterate or intentionally mysterious, *LD* is a complicated book. It's not easy. And there's this thin line between flawed and intentionally rigorous. You gotta work a little to really get what's happening at the end and the beginning. My hope is that even if you don't really "get it" there might be enough for you to go back and reread and enjoy other parts.

SG: In the title essay of your collection, "How to Slowly Kill Yourself and Others in America," you wrote:

"I think I want to hurt myself more than I'm already hurting. I'm not the smartest boy in the world by a long shot, but even in my funk I know that easy remedies like eating your way out of sad, or fucking your way out of sad, or lying your way out of sad, or slanging your way out of sad, or robbing your way out of sad, or gambling your way out of sad, or shooting your way out of sad, are just slower, more acceptable ways for desperate folks, and especially paroled black boys in our country, to kill ourselves and others close to us in America."

You write about feelings, talk about them and share them, that ain't what men do, especially not Black men. How important is emotion to your work? To writing in general?

KL: Emotion, like race, is in every sentence ever created. It's important that we own that and explore that. Folk who identity as men in this country are encouraged often to be cold and not regretful. That's the hallmark of evil. We have all hurt ourselves, and more importantly, hurt other folks who we should not have hurt. If we say we don't regret anything, we're saying that we don't give a fuck for hurting folks who should not have been hurt. If I was the God of classes and relationships, I'd start every class and relationship on earth with the questions: "What do you regret?," "How do you want to be loved?," "How do you deserve to be loved?," "How do you imagine your most loving self would be different from who you are today?"

SG: If you could make a mixtape for every writer out there taking you up on your call to practice, what five songs would absolutely have to be on it?

KL: Wow. Best interview ever. Okay, today I'd go with Mahalia Jackson's "How I Got Over" and Halona King's "Monster in the Night" and Jigga's "Public Service Announcement" and Outkast's "Ova da Wudz" and Jill Scott's "Hate on Me." Thank you for being way beyond wonderful.

Heavy Are the Words of Kiese Laymon

Auburn Avenue / 2018

From *Auburn Avenue*, Autumn/Winter 2018. Reprinted with permission of *Auburn Avenue*.

Interviewer: You were born and raised in Jackson, Mississippi. Like many parts of the South, Mississippi is known for its shameful history of racism, but also for the indisputable fortitude of people of African descent. How would you describe your relationship with your homeland?

Kiese Laymon: I feel really lucky to be born and raised in the South, particularly in Jackson, Mississippi. I grew up aware that white people lived in my state and really had most of the power, but Jackson is a predominately Black city, so I thought the state had a lot of Black people. When I grew up, I found out that was not true. For a writer or artist, it's one of the best places in the world to grow up. There's such a rich history of art—literary art and visual art. One of the reasons I think it's so rich is because of the robust forces in my state that brutalize people. I think the clash of people that want to harm vulnerable people, and the fact that vulnerable people often create art in the face of that harm, makes my state special to me.

I: In the beginning of *Heavy*, you write, "I wanted to write a lie." Why do you think lies have so much power in influencing decisions and thoughts?

KL: I just think lies are easier. It's easier to walk through life believing A when B is true, or when both A and B may be true. It's easier to make money if you lie. It's easier to get people to like you if you lie. I think corporations encourage this. With the book, I think people wanted to read one of those stories that ends with everything being hunky-dory. Like, "I lost all this weight . . . my family lost weight and we came to the conclusion that to be healthy in this country, all we need to do is eat right and talk to each other a little bit more. . . ." Maybe. But there's a lot of nasty stuff too and I wanted to write about a lot of that.

I: Certainly the task of writing *Heavy* must have been tough at times. How did you find the courage and emotional capacity necessary to reflect on your past?

KL: I found the courage by writing two other books—two other books that were really different from this book. Those books were important and I honed my skills with them. I had to have a particular kind of skillset to write *Heavy*. That's why I couldn't create the book for two decades. I didn't know how to enter into some of those memories. I didn't know how to use the right adjectives and page breaks. Once I got my skills right, that helped build my courage. I had to write a lot to get the skill to create it.

I: The memoir recounts your life from your childhood to adulthood. What would say to the child-version Kiese?

KL: I would say, as much as possible, never lie—never lie to himself or to people that he loves. And get some sleep 'cause this life shit is no joke.

I: *Heavy* is dubbed "An American Memoir." Surely the events and moments detailed in the book have shaped your identity. How do you currently define your identity, particularly your "Americanness?"

KL: I'm a Black American writer from the South. I'm not one of these "rah-rah American" type of people. I'm a very "rah-rah Black American" type of person. I don't understand patriotism. I just don't understand it. "American" is a very nuanced word to me. Some people just want to focus on the positives of that word and not the terrifying things about the word. I'm an American—I'm not proud of that and I'm not spiteful of it either. It's a brutal mix of a lot of stuff. I don't think we spend enough time thinking about the brutality of the nation and the ways in which it has seeped into all of us. When I call *Heavy* "An American Memoir," I'm saying, "This is an American story. It's critical of the nation. It's also embracing of the nation." Ultimately it's saying, "We've got to do better, or else . . ." and actually, I think we've already met the "or else. . . ."

I: Can you talk about the significance that Black women had in shaping you and your worldview?

KL: Generally, in my life and in the lives of Black men that I grew up with, Black women were the only people on which we could rely. But sometimes when you say that, it's easy for people to see Black women as perfect. One of the things I'm showing in the book is that one of the ways you love people is to show them what you remember about them. In that memory there's going to be some wonderful stuff, but because they're people, there's going to be some not-so-wonderful stuff too. In general, I would say Black women have taught me how to read, how to write, how to love, how to listen. If I'm also being honest, some of the Black women in my family—because they were dealing with a lack of love from the nation, Black men, and white folks—were also harmful and abusive. In my family, sometimes the people that were the kindest and the most generous and impactful to me were also harmful. I'm talking specifically about my mom. Thankfully, she tried to instill in me the importance of revision, which means that I look back at the way she parented, the way I was as a child, and how I've chosen to live in this world. That's a gift from her. It's complicated. At the end of the day, Black women are not magical, but they have held this country down, in spite of the way it has treated them.

I: The memoir's title, *Heavy*, can be used to describe the subject matter of the book, some of the events in your life, and even your physical weight as a child. One of the definitions of "heavy" is "something of a great weight." What is the "heaviest" thing about Kiese Laymon?

KL: I would say the heaviest things about me are my memory and my imagination. They're far heavier than my body, far heavier than my relationship with my state, my nation, and my mama.

I: In the memoir, you talk about your early relationship with books and language. Can you expound on this early impact that written language had in your life?

KL: My mom had me at a young age. She was a student and was always into books, so they were always around. Because they were around, I was never intimidated by them. I read a lot, but I really didn't like books because they kept me from being outside with my friends. My mama made me read and write before I could do anything I wanted to do. She wanted me to read all the white canonical books. She thought that if I mastered that kind of stuff, I would be safer in the country and in the world. I always knew I'd write books, but I never thought they would be good books. When you have so many of them in your house, you realize most aren't good. I figured I could write some bad ones. But reading books by Baldwin, Toni Cade Bambara, Richard Wright really make my memory and imagination so heavy. I see what people like that did with their memory and imagination and it makes you know what is possible. It gives you goals and lets you know that there's something possible beyond the goal and beyond your imagination, if that's even a place. I just always seek to go there.

I: What is one of the more recent lessons that you have learned about yourself?

KL: The same thing that made me gain 150 lbs. is the same thing that made me lose damn near 200 lbs. That same thing made me able to write *Heavy*, *Long Division*, and *How to Slowly Kill Yourself and Others in America*. When I'm writing, I'm obsessive about the line, the break, and what I'm doing with chapters and characters. That obsessive compulsion can be used in wonderful ways but can also be used in ways that are completely harmful. Thankfully, I can use writing to explore the compulsion. But I didn't really accept that until I finished this book.

I: Does that impact how do you deal with making your personal writing available to the public?

KL: I'm like an obsessive reviser, so it makes editors really upset. For example, the book was done and then I did the audiobook. I saw sentences and words that I wanted to change, so I did. In a way, I think that's good but I don't know how to let anything go. So *Heavy* is out in the world now, but when I read over it, there's a whole lot of stuff that I want to change. What I have to do is save that editing for the next book.

I: Why do you think people should read *Heavy*?

KL: We see a lot of books where fathers are writing to sons, mothers are writing to daughters, and parents in general are writing to their children, but don't see Black child writing to black parent. I think *Heavy* is a new kind of book—not that it's completely innovative, but there are some things that you're going to read in it that you've never read before. I also think people should read it so they can write their own versions of it. I hope people see it as a weighted look into themselves. It's hard and it might not be for everybody, but for folks that really want to do the work and see a model of how to talk to people that raised them, how to talk to themselves, and how to be honest without being obsessed with progress, I think it's a good book for them.

I: In fifty to a hundred years from now, what do you want people to understand about you?

KL: I just want people to care about the work. It's difficult because the work, on the surface, is so much about me. But in the work, I'm laying out what I see as the cracks of who I am. There's a really hyperbolic "I" in the book, but it's so connected to a "we." I want people to say he created some art and really did some work for us.

Writing Back to History: A Conversation with Kiese Laymon

Monet Patrice Thomas / 2018

From *The Rumpus*, October 2018. Reprinted with permission.

In the aptly titled memoir, *Heavy: An American Memoir*, Kiese Laymon, the Ottilie Schillig Professor of English and Creative Writing at the University of Mississippi and author of a novel, *Long Division*, and a collection of essays, *How to Slowly Kill Yourself and Others in America*, does not shy away from the difficult truths plaguing himself and the people around him. From sexual and physical abuse to income inequality, to body image, addiction, and systemic racism, Laymon compels us as readers to interrogate our own dark corners. Like James Baldwin, and more recently like Ta-Nehisi Coates, Laymon uses direct address, but unlike those men, he speaks to a woman—his mother, and sometimes his grandmother—about the ways in which their expressions of love for each other have failed. His message evolves to include us all, firstly Black folks, and then the nation at large, with unflinching candor in an attempt to jolt us into action. Alexander Chee says, "*Heavy* is a gift to us, if we can pick it up—a moral exercise and an intimate history that is at the same time a story about America."

I caught up with Professor Laymon about the difference between invented history versus real history, the distinctly different tone of *Heavy*, and why humor is an inherently Black trait.

The Rumpus: Earlier this year I read a self-help book called *The Big Leap* about how we hold ourselves back from reaching our true potential, and in it the author, Gay Hendricks, lists the top five reasons *why* we hold ourselves back and one of those reasons was "fear of embarrassing or shaming our family," and I thought that in order for you to write this book that was something you had to overcome, because Black children are often taught very early that everything we do outside our home is a reflection on our home.

Laymon: Because one of the things that's more embarrassing, not just to our parents, but also to ourselves is if someone goes out of the house and tells the truth about something we did in the house. That can be more embarrassing than people lying on me, but that's where it all comes full circle. My grandmama raised me; my mother made me into a writer. Writing is how I deal with the world and we have just gotten to a place in my family, in particular, with my mother, and even in the nation where I'm just trying to use everything in my disposal to be a better person, a better grandson, a better son, a better partner. My mother and I were just in a really bad situation and I wanted to use writing to help us. Not that writing could get us out, but it could get us closer, help us find a way into memories that we always tried to evade.

And to do that I had to write things that could potentially be embarrassing to me, but also for my mother, but I tried not to write anything about her that I didn't see. And she did read it before it went out. I didn't want to embarrass anyone. I wanted to try to love everyone in that book, especially my mom and my grandmama. Sometimes I think really loving people artistically can be harmful. This is not just a collection of confessions; it's a piece of art I made for my mother and whatever comes from people indulging in that art is something I'll have to deal with. And on one level this is like when I was a kid and I went to school and the teacher gave me construction paper and I had to make some shit for my family. I remember on those days my mother was crazy happy, because I gave her some picture that was probably terrible, but she loved it. So this book is like another piece of art I wanted her to have.

Rumpus: The tone here is so different from your other work. It's gentler. In your nonfiction collection of essays, *How to Slowly Kill Yourself and Others in America*, there's a lot more anger. I wondered if that shift happened because you're speaking to your mother.

Laymon: Beyond wanting to write a heart-to-heart with my mother, as an artist I just didn't want to write the same book again. In my mind I was always writing four books that were for Black kids. *Long Division* was supposed to be two books. And this was going to be my last book, but tonally I wanted it to be different. And for sure I was hoping it would be different, because the last thing you want people to say is, *I already read this book by this author*. There's an attempt at tenderness and also an attempt to write into places I was afraid to write about at any other time in my life. I wanted to write about the terror I felt growing up with my mother and I wanted to write about the absolutely sublime joy. I wanted to write about those places

I don't even know what to do with, you know what I'm saying? My mother had me young and by the time I was twelve grown men were coming up to me and asking me to hook them up with my sister, which is why that first scene is with us at the casino and her telling me to pretend to be her husband. There was an intense level of intimacy. So I needed to be as tender as I could while also being as honest as I could.

Rumpus: I couldn't recall another time I'd read a memoir from a man, particularly from a Black man and presumably a straight Black man, with this much vulnerability. And it made me wonder if we allow Black men this level of vulnerability. It's almost not safe. It's a question of who gets to be vulnerable.

Laymon: That's an interesting way you posed that because I'm thinking about permission. You said "gets to," and I'm not sure if we're not given permission or if we opt out or both. I think about the direct address books I read, and if they're written by men they're usually written to a son or a daughter. Baldwin wrote to his nephew. But I think we love thinking about Black men as father figures because we're obsessed with this notion of Black men being absent fathers. That's fine, I appreciate that art, but to tap into the emotional reservoir I had to write this to my mother. I wrote a million drafts and when I really thought I had it was when I had four sections: one was to my grandma, one was to my mother, one was to my imaginary daughter who I don't have, and one was to my ex-partner who I'd harmed. But the hardest section to write was to my mom. That allowed me to be more vulnerable, but also she gave me my political imagination and she gave me my writing practice, so if I was going to be tender, if I was going be afraid and write a book that was reaching out to her and to us and really beckon us to be more radically kind to one another, I just had to write it to her. I didn't know how to write that book to a general reader.

Rumpus: I kept coming back to your middle school teacher talking about Eudora Welty and how you rip apart her argument about "quirky racism" being in the past, but then also feeling a tug toward the interior of Welty's stories. And I think that highlights a really common contrasting emotion readers and writers of color experience about the canon—that it's not for us and yet we learn from it. Do we burn down the canon? Is there anything in the canon worth keeping?

Laymon: Oh yeah. For sure. It's all worth keeping. But we shouldn't call it the canon. If you have all kinds of people but only value the work of green people and then you call the work of green people the canon, then I think years later you don't have to destroy the books, but you do have to destroy the designation. I had to read all those books several times, but as a reader I know there's so much more. I don't even know what the purpose of the canon is. I've found a lot of usefulness in Faulkner, but the Mississippi he describes is a version of Mississippi. The words he uses—he could not describe the Jackson I grew up in and use those same words. He couldn't write about it all because it's too Black and it's not filled with Black people working for him or giving him the respect he thinks he deserves. And I think Faulkner is one of the top twenty prose writers ever, but the usefulness is that I can go in and dismantle it. When people read *Heavy* thirty to forty years from now, it's usefulness won't be in reading it and saying, "I appreciate this," but the usefulness will be in some writer, hopefully from Mississippi, who will tear the book up and be like, *I see what he's attempting to do, but this is bullshit and he didn't pull it off here.*

When the word "canon" is used we're supposed to have this referential appreciation. And I love Eudora Welty but she's an artist and I think she'd want us to get up in there and mess around with her stuff. Tinker with it. Tell the world where it goes wrong. And because I'm not a literary critic, I critique the work by creating alternative work. So my book is absolutely a critique of *Black Boy*, absolutely a critique of *A Good Man Is Hard to Find* or *Go Down, Moses* or *Absalom, Absalom!* I'm thankful for that work and because of that love it means I'm going to get down and do something they didn't do.

Rumpus: Well, talking about Mississippi and Faulkner leads to me to another writer who I love: Jesmyn Ward. She writes about Mississippi and she was the first writer who made me feel less embarrassed about my own Southern roots. And *Heavy* did that for me, too: talking about place, talking about what it means to be Southern without any signposts, and just reckoning with what it means to be Black from the South. Is it easier to be in Mississippi? Or is it easier to be away writing about it?

Laymon: I'm from Jackson, which is the capital of Mississippi, and it's the Blackest city in the state. It's eighty-five percent Black and that's where I was born and where I was raised. Early on a lot of the Black writers who could leave left. And then I left, for my life and for my health. I was in New York for fourteen years, which is the longest I'd been in one place, but I knew I needed to come home. I'm not sure what that meant. Was home Jackson? Was home my grandmama's house? Was it my grandmama's porch? I got a lot of job offers and I decided to come to the University of Mississippi because of the program and the department. I think we have the best English department and creative writing department in the country. And I do think Mississippi is the best state in the Union. Mississippi is responsible for so much of what we people use but don't understand—whether it's music or sense of morality or our particular kind of organized protest. But last night I was thinking maybe I came home just to write this book.

Rumpus: Baldwin wrote, in one section of *The Fire Next Time*:

"The paradox—and a fearful paradox it is—is that the American Negro can have no future anywhere, on any continent, as long as he is unwilling to accept his past. To accept one's past—one's history—is not the same thing as drowning in it; it is learning how to use it. An invented past can never be used; it cracks and crumbles under the pressures of life like clay in a season of drought."

And this quote came back to me because this book seemed like how you worked through your own past.

Kiese: Oh absolutely. Baldwin's work, definitely *The Fire Next Time* and *Giovanni's Room*, were guides to me. I think the line between an invented history and "real" history is so thin. In some ways all writing is invented. It's an artful rendering of memory. You have to be careful in the way some kinds of inventions are necessary. Some people conflate memoir with autobiography or a tell-all. This is not an attempt at me telling everything there is about myself. It's an attempt to create art out of the parts of my past that I'm most afraid of and it's also a call to arms to the nation to slow down with these progress narratives. Progress at the expense of honest reckoning is often terror for a whole lot of people. And that's where we are now. Not just politically, but also within our families—at least in my family. When I first started writing this book it was supposed to be a weight loss book. I was supposed to be trying to lose one hundred and fifty pounds while talking to my grandma and my mother and my aunts and their relationship with weight and sexual violence.

Rumpus: Wait! Really?

Laymon: Yeah, that's the book I sold. And I wrote that book. Which is why in the opening I say, "I wanted to write to you. . . ." And then one day I was talking to my grandmama and she started describing a memory that we had already talked about for the book, which I had recorded, but it was different, so I said, "Grandmama, why you lying? That's not what happened. That's not the story you told me." And she said, "Kie, I told you a lie because you're writing it for a book. I'm not going to tell you the truth because you're going to put in a book." At that point I was like, *I need to write back to them and to that.* That first book, about weight loss, Black folks would've clapped for being alive but it wasn't a book that did anything to my insides or anyone else's insides, so that's why I decided to write back to my family after talking to them about their experiences and their bodies and their food and the way they survived different kinds of violences. History, for me, and the past, as everybody says, is always present, but it's also an opportunity for love. I think about all the times I was the most deceitful in my relationships, it's because someone loved me and really wanted to know me and where I've been, but I just didn't have the courage to walk back there with them. One, I didn't trust if I walked back there with them that they would still love me and only in retrospect did I get, *Oh, this person loved me and wanted to know where I've been.* And two, I thought I loved them enough to know where they've been, but if I couldn't honestly talk about where I've been then could I really hold places they've been? So with *Heavy* I really wanted to explore that dynamic a little bit more: can you love people if you're not willing to see where they've been and also share where they've been? And that's not drowning, like Baldwin mentions; that's opening the door for radical conversation, which leads to radical relationships and ultimately to liberation. And that's the question the book is asking: Are we ready to really love each other? The civil rights movement would've been a lot stronger if the men were able to reckon with the harm they did. So this is not a completely political tool, but I do think if we tighten up on our familial relationships and allow for an attempt at honesty, we'll be better as people and as families and better as political forces.

Rumpus: Did you know your mother was going to write a response?

Laymon: Initially, she wrote an essay that was going to be in the book. But when I first finished the book, I had no idea what it would mean. Then she read the book and wrote her response and I was overwhelmed. Overwhelmed with joy. My mom and I, we've been through it. There were times when you couldn't convince me that my mother had it in her to love me. Because it got to a point where love meant "Watch out for the police, Kie," or "Don't eat sugar or carbs, Kie," and other warnings, but there's a lot of other shit we needed to be talking about besides the police getting to me or me eating too much. There are several layers to *Heavy*, but on the most basic level this is me asking my mother for help. Life was eating my ass up. And I needed help. So when she wrote that letter with the parts where she says publicly, "I should've done this. Or I should've said that," as a woman obsessed with progress, that she wished she could go back and make different decisions to better the quality of our relationship was huge. We also talked about gambling, which is eating up both sides of my family, and the shame that's there because we come from a family of hard labor and often we take from that labor and throw it away. And I think a lot of us feel like we don't deserve that money and a lot of us are earning less than we should for our labor. But yeah, that letter was one of the best things. I couldn't believe that she'd taken the art I'd made her seriously.

Rumpus: In all its seriousness, *Heavy* has genuinely funny moments. I had to stop several times, because I was laughing so hard. But then I realized that the laughter usually came either before or after something intense or even in a moment of intensity, and I think that's a very deeply Black trait. I'm curious if you see humor as a defense mechanism?

Laymon: It's definitely part defense mechanism. In *Heavy*, humor is a way for me to write into what people call trauma. I didn't want to use the word "trauma" in the book, but the most violent and traumatic times in my life—when I recall them, I laugh. Like when Black people talk about being beaten all you have to do is say, *Man when I was thirteen my mother took an extension cord and she beat me across the head* . . . and most Black people I know will start laughing. But we're not laughing at that person or presuming that person deserved it; it's a way of allowing us into what was obviously painful and traumatic. I don't ever think of it as humor OR violence, the way I don't think of things as love OR tragedy. All of those things mingle. And when I write I want all of those things as honestly as possible, to find the comedic slivers within something that was absolutely terrifying. We need the comedic to allow us into the memory.

"A Reckoning Is Different Than a Tell-All": An Interview with Kiese Laymon

Abigail Bereola / 2018

From *The Paris Review*, October 18, 2018. Reprinted with permission.

Interviewer: What does heaviness evoke for you?

Kiese Laymon: Heaviness evokes fear and desperation and, most importantly, a soulfulness. For me, it's not one thing. I think I thought it was one thing before I started the book, but as I worked on it, I began to embrace the soulfulness in heaviness. It's something most people try to avoid, but it's also something that I need to make it through the day.

I: You write this book to your mother, telling her some of what made you and broke you, telling her some of where you've been and where you want to go. You say that you would rather write a lie and you know that she would rather have you write one. Sometimes it made me feel like I was looking at something that wasn't meant for me, that was intensely private. Why did you decide to write to her?

KL: I was at a point in my life where the closest I could get to honesty was talking to her because of so many lies between the two of us, so many things I didn't say. And you know, my mama is a Black woman from the South—from Mississippi. She's a teacher. She loves Black people. She's an American. So she occupies all these subject positions that I wanted to talk to in this book, and I just didn't want to write a book about my mama that wasn't written to my mama. Do you know what I mean? I think people conflate memoir with autobiography a lot, but memoir is the artful rendering of an experience. For me, to get to the artfulness of it, I had to think of a person who could help me keep the good fat and cut out the bad fat. And thinking about what my mama would want to hear and not want to hear helped me do that. But the real reason is that we had been lying to each other for my whole life and I didn't want to do that anymore.

I: I kept coming back to this thought while reading, about the difference between a tell-all and a memoir. I didn't feel like your book was a tell-all—I definitely felt like there were some things that you were keeping for yourself and for your family and for the people that you've known.

KL: Oh, for sure. I'm glad you say that. You know, I'm Black and from Mississippi. My people do not play that tell-all-your-business-type stuff. But at the same time, I think there are some things we do need to talk about and reckon with. A reckoning, I think, is different than a tell-all. And the book that you read—not only is it heavily revised, but there's a lot of stuff that I took out because my family was like, "Okay, that's not something that people get to see." And there were people in my life that I'd harmed—I tried to write about that harm, because I thought that was the right thing to do. And some of those people were just like, "Naw, you don't get to harm me and then ultimately get paid for harming me." You know what I'm saying? So I had to take some other sections out of the book just because ethically it was wrong. But it was important for me to write it all out. All the stuff I'm talking about is in the subtext of the book. In a tell-all, I don't think there's much subtext. Everything is just explicit. I think there's a ton of subtext in *Heavy* and I think people will know the emotional registers that I'm trying to play with. Though I give people way more, probably, than they deserve, to tell you the truth, just in terms of my information about me. But you know, whatever. I gotta sit in that. I gotta deal with that.

I: Has there been a dissonance between writing for your mom but knowing that all these other people are going to read it? Did you have to write it to your mom to write it?

KL: I had to write it to my mom to write it. It was a different book initially. It was a weight-loss book. I was talking to my mom and my grandmom and my aunt and other people close to me about their relationships to weight and food and sexual violence. It was more of a reported book, and then a few things happened. People in my family were just lying. And I'm into language, so if you lie, that's not a big deal, I'm still captivated by the language we use to tell lies, but at one point, I was just like, "Why y'all lying?" And they were just like, "Uh, 'cause it's going in a book. Duh." They were just like, "Why are you asking me? I'm lying because you're trying to tell everybody our business." And then I was just like, "You know what? I need to write back to them instead of just writing about them."

And so initially, one section was written to my grandma, one section was written to my ma, one section was written to a partner that I had a long time ago, and one section was written to my daughter. I mean an imaginary daughter—I don't have a daughter. I don't have any children. So I wrote that draft and I kept thinking about what I didn't say, what I didn't write, what I couldn't write, and then I was just like, "Man, I'm scared to write this to the person I need to write it to." And that was my mama. I wrote it: draft, redraft, redraft. And then I showed it to her and we started having these conversations about lots of things we hadn't talked about, particularly about addiction and violence. I went back and revised it again. I just needed my mama to get me through this. And my mama was the one who taught me how to write. My mama definitely would prefer me not to write this kind of book for lots of reasons, but in a lot of ways, she made me. She created me, but she also gave me my writing practice. So I just thought it made sense for this book to really be written to the person that I think made me, and also the person who I'm most like in ways that are great and also ways that maybe aren't so great.

I: In centering survival, it seems like you also had a childhood that centered whiteness in some ways. A lot of things were about what white people thought or what white people would do to you. What does that do to a young Black boy or young Black girl?

KL: I think it does exactly what it does. It's weird because I grew up in a super-Black house, super-Black neighborhood, super-Black communities, but this anxiety about white folks and what they would do if given opportunity was always around us, even before I went to white schools. Part of that is because I live in Mississippi, and the history of us and white folk is a brutal history, but I think sometimes it can inadvertently make white folks into the traffic cops of your life. It's like what my mom always used to say, "You gotta be twice as good as white folks," and I'm just like, "But they're not even that excellent. Why are you trying to tell me to center some people that aren't that excellent in my estimation?"

It makes us ignore the contours of our own imagination and our experiences. And I understand—it's America. Everything is a big gumbo. But for me, I think it makes it harder for us to imagine because we're literally told that if we imagine out of the box, white people are gon' get us. And so when I bring that shit up in the book, I'm not trying to indict my grandmom, my mama, and them, because I understand. They're trying to protect themselves and protect their child and their grandchild. I think that's what a lot of Black parents all over the world—definitely in the Deep South—do. But my thing is I don't know. Do white people always have to be present? Another reason I wrote to my mama was because I'm just tired of reading books where Black people talk to white folks about white folks. I do think there's a difference between writing a book to white people and writing a book that's partially about the communicative gesture of always talking about white people to Black folks. I just hate when I go to a speech or a talk and it's a Black person and they're talking to a majority-white audience. There's so many things that have to be synthesized and explained and it's always cornier than it needs to be. I think there's a pressure to write that kind of book and write those kinds of essays, and Lord knows those books and essays pay, but I ain't wanna do that shit. I just didn't wanna do that.

I: I grappled with this a lot in college in particular. I remember watching a play called *Word Becomes Flesh*, by Marc Bamuthi Joseph. It's a series of letters from a Black man to his unborn son that uses hip-hop, dance, and music. The audience watching the play was mostly white, and I just remember feeling like they were laughing at all the wrong parts.

KL: Yeah, we all been there. Brutal.

I: I was just like, it's great that this is touring and it was really important for me to see it, but what does it mean when Black art needs white dollars to be sustainable?

KL: That's the question. That's it. And if you expand it beyond what we traditionally call art—writing and dance and performance—if you think about the art of human being, what does it mean that in this country, in order to be sustainable, there's a performative aspect to all of us? Not everybody, but most of us are performing—no matter how radical we are or claim to be, there's a level of performance for white dollars. My grandmom performed that shit in the chicken plant. I often perform it in a fucking classroom or when I go to talk about my book. My mama, when she goes in the grocery store, she has to do a particular kind of performance for white folk in order to make it out of the grocery store, in order to make it home. I had a lot, a lot, a lot of experiences with police that were just terrible and violent and I didn't want to bring those into that book—I just wanted to allude to them, and the one episode that's in there is with my mom, because I feel like sometimes we don't think about the way Black women encounter police, and the way Black women who have children—not just Black boys, but children—have to navigate police situations. It's a performance, sometimes, just to make it home. And then you see somebody like Sandra Bland who was trying to do the performance. She'd been trained like we all had and she still didn't make it home.

I: You once said in an interview that your mother equated survival with joy. That sentiment feels like it's all over this book. But in that same interview, you say that you don't believe survival and joy are the same thing. Do you feel that you've found joy?

KL: I feel joyful having this conversation. I'm definitely beyond thinking about joy as this permanent destination the way I used to. I used to think about joy as a deliverance, like, I'm gonna be joyful, I'm gonna feel joyful. Now I think I'm more about, just, being able to articulate the times when I do feel immense joy. Like probably thirty minutes ago, the long list for fiction came out for the National Book Award and I mean, shit, I felt something beyond joy to see Jamel Brinkley and Nafissa Thompson-Spires and Tayari Jones there where they're supposed to be. I think sometimes when you grow up the way a lot of us grew up, when the things that are supposed to happen actually do happen, you feel joy. We should live in a world where it's like, *Of course those books are on the long list*. But it's like when Serena Williams plays. My family's just stuck at the TV because of course! She's the greatest fucking athlete of whenever, but then of course she's going to be treated like shit. Because she's a Black woman. And so, that makes the joy of watching her win so much better. I'm able to articulate joy a little bit more, but I definitely used to think, *Man, I feel kind of sad*. I feel kind of in a funk. And if I could just make it to joy, everything'll be all right. Or I used to be like, *If my book gets published, Imma be joyful*, or, *If I get such and such, but my life ain't like that*. There's some joyful shit every day, but I ain't reached that joy as a destination point. I don't think that exists, actually. Not for me.

I: That's an interesting distinction. Not that it doesn't exist at all, but just for you.

KL: Yeah, definitely. I think it definitely exists.

I: In the book, there exists a duality between love and violence, between an unbreakable companionship and beatings and manipulation. In *All about Love*, bell hooks says, "No one can rightfully claim to be loving when behaving abusively." Do you think violence and love can coexist?

KL: I think love exists to confront violence—emotional violence, geographic violence, race violence, gendered violence. So yeah, I think they definitely coexist because love is always attempting not to smother violence, but to disarm violence in some way. And I think we often use violence as a backlash to love. Like Baldwin always says, and like Morrison teaches us, love is not pure. It's dirty and it's necessarily stanky and funky.

I: In some ways, it seems like love can be a finite resource when you're strapped for other things. If you have to worry about keeping a roof over your head and how much money you'll have for the rest of the month and whether there's food in the fridge, you may not have the space to learn how to love well. Do you think learning to love well is a luxury?

KL: I actually don't think that. I don't think there's any way in the world I would be like, *Most of the people I met who have an abundance of stuff are better at loving.* Everything that they encourage us to have as Black folk—be in a two-parent home, go to "the best schools," have money in your home—everything that we supposedly want or have been taught to want and need, that dude Donald Trump had. That motherfucker is terrible at loving, as are the people who elected him. So I don't know if it's a luxury.

I: You write that your mom never wanted you to let white folks see you fail. Do you still worry about that? Does she?

KL: She definitely does. Me, not as much. And that brings me joy. I can definitely say at this point in my life, I'm cool failing in front of white folks. And that failure could manifest in walking into a hotel filled with white people and tripping. I dress how I want to dress all the time now in my life, I talk how I want to talk. But it's a paradox. I'm not wealthy, so I also need money and I know that if I cut up too much, Imma cut my check. You know? And if I cut my check, my grandmama not gon' have the health care she needs next month and my mama might not have this and my auntie might not have that. So I'm not tryna front like I'm all liberated and shit, but I kinda sorta don't give a fuck about what they think about me in the moment. But my mother absolutely, absolutely, absolutely cares about that and I understand why. My grandmother too.

I: Do you feel like the not caring allows for a freedom of humanity that the desperation of caring doesn't?

KL: I do. I definitely think that. And it's not just not caring. For me, it's about what I actually do care about. So my mother, for example, doesn't want me to have the word ain't in anything I write. She might not love that word, but also, she still might be like, "You know, Kie, if they see you writing that, they're not going to think you're blah blah blah, and if they think you're not intellectually capable, you're going to limit your economic options in the future." And what I'm trying to tell my mama is that I am an artist, so when I'm writing a line that one character is saying, "I ain't going," and the other character is saying, "How come?" and another character be like, "'Cuz I don't want to,'" that to me is not performing for white people. It's trying to honor the rhetorical discursive tradition that made us. That's not just about, Imma do this 'cuz white people want me or don't want me to. That's actually about what we talked about earlier in terms of centering. I just want to try to rigorously honor the words and the sentences that made us. That's a big part of what I'm trying to do in my work.

I: You've said that this book was you asking your mom for help. What has been the result of her reading it?

KL: Initially, her response was going to be the last chapter, but then we decided not to do that, so on my blog, she wrote a response to the book. What she wrote in there was something I'd just never thought my mom would say publicly. She admits to certain things that I never thought she would. We've had conversations that we never thought we would have. But it's not like it's all good now. It's better—it's definitely better. I just think it's important for us to have the words love and violence and addiction and joy. It means a lot to be able to talk to my mama about the ways I've harmed and failed at life, too, because I'm just a private person in a way, even though I write a lot of shit that's not private. And I think it helps her see her son, maybe for the first time really. Honestly. And I think that's really scary for my mama. Definitely scary for me.

Kiese Laymon: "Absent Fathers and Present Mothers"

Poppy Noor / 2018

From *The Guardian*, November 24, 2018. © Guardian News & Media Ltd 2024.

Poppy Noor: You were raised by women—your mother and grandma—how was that?

Kiese Laymon: We hear about absent fathers but not present mothers. A present father wouldn't have helped me at all, if he was modelling harmful behavior daily. My grandmother, mother, and aunt were pretty good at loving. They tried. They failed often. But their ability to love is why I'm talking to you today. My book is all about love. We can talk about the difference between Black and white or Democrats and Republicans but if we don't learn to love the people we purport to love, we have no chance. Trump says he loves America. Is there any proof of that? No. There's absolutely no proof that that man loves America.

PN: Would Trump be a better man if he was raised by women?

KL: One of the most useful things that people like Kavanaugh and Trump show us is that having lots of money, a two-parent family, and going to the best schools doesn't necessarily produce the best men.

PN: Your mother wanted to protect you from the things that can happen to Black boys—incarceration, gang violence, police violence. But in the end that harms you, too . . . .

KL: White people in the US have been so violent to Black folk, and there is a belief that if we present ourselves as perfect, we have a better chance of coming home, of not suffering, of getting more access to healthy choices and second chances. As a kid it struck me that Martin Luther King was dressed really well when he got murdered. Obama epitomizes what my mom wanted me to be. She wanted me to be skinny, to talk like Obama, she wanted me to never confront white people in any sort of abrasive way. But people still called Obama a radical, said he was a Muslim and a terrorist. History says to me that respectable excellence does not liberate Black people.

PN: You write about personal struggles—sexual violence, addiction, abuse. Which was the hardest to address?

KL: The gambling addiction that me and my mother had. The book starts with us raking up quarters on a casino floor, at a time when I had no concept of what an addiction is, and it's the best feeling in the world. It ends with us reckoning with that addiction. We were working really hard to accumulate money that our family needed. And we were literally giving it all away.

PN: You were 210 lbs. at ten and 319 lbs. by the time you were at university. Then you began to starve yourself. Tell me about being a man with an eating disorder . . . .

KL: When I was a child, and later at grad school, I was gorging—looking for pizza in dorm bins, eating hunny-bun after hunny-bun, going to an all-you-can-eat buffet followed by a Dunkin' Donuts. I still feel shame talking about that. But the scary thing is that, when I talk about when I starved myself I don't feel embarrassed. Even though I was eating one meal every three days, the most unhealthy I'd ever been. I almost want you to know what I was capable of doing. Eating disorders aren't flagged up for all people in the same way. When I was excessively working out, there would be skinny men in the gym, skinny gender-queer people, skinny Black and brown folk. . . . But the people who got pointed out as "anorexic" or "bulimic" were always white women. People would say, "Someone needs to stop her coming in here," and I'd think, she's not even the skinniest person in here! I'm interested in why we can see disordered eating in white women, but not other people.

PN: How did it feel when you were shortlisted for the Andrew Carnegie medal and the Kirkus prize?

KL: The first thing I wrote came out when I was thirty-eight [he is forty-four now]. That is not young for a writer. I have such mistrust of the awarding systems in general. So there's a part of me that thought, did I do something wrong? Maybe I didn't do my art the way I thought I did it.

PN: What books are on your bedside table?

KL: I can't tell you the name yet but it's by one of my friends. It's a letter to her two sons and it's amazing. It came right on time. Sometimes with these epistolary books it's easy to be really cheesy, really formulaic—the letter form can lend itself to a kind of one-dimensionality, but this writer manages to texture herself and her boys in really distinct ways. She does more than just lament or try to give them wisdom. She's telling a complicated story about who they are, why they're like that, and where she thinks they should go.

PN: Are there any genres you avoid?

KL: I don't read books about the economy. I think some of those economists try to be brave but mostly they don't write books for people like me.

PN: Who is your favorite villain or hero in a book?

KL: Today I'm teaching Nafissa Thompson-Spires's *Heads of the Colored People*. There's a character called Riley who I'm obsessed with. Riley is Black, and the first sentence goes: "Riley wore blue contact lenses and bleached his hair—which he worked with gel and a blow-dryer and a flatiron some mornings into Sonic the Hedgehog spikes so stiff you could prick your fingers on them." You see immediately that Riley's a character most of us have never read in American literature. In Paul Beatty's *White Boy Shuffle*, Nicholas Scoby is one of the best secondary characters I've ever read. This white kid who becomes a basketball phenomenon because he never misses a shot. And when he finally does, he has to kill himself. He's obsessed with [Charles] Mingus and jazz and Asian American film in the mid-1930s. I love shit that's super-soulful. If you can tantalize the soulful parts and the more traditional parts of me, I love that.

"I Don't Want People to Forget the Sentence": An Interview with Kiese Laymon

Meghan Brown / 2019

Originally appeared in January 2019. Reprinted by permission of Oxford University Press on behalf of The Society for the Study of the Multi-Ethnic Literature of the United States.

Meghan Brown: I want to get started by talking about music. In your "Author's Note" to *How to Slowly Kill Yourself and Others in America*, you write that you "thought of the essays as tracks" (13). How has musical form influenced your writing?

Kiese Laymon: With the essay collection, I wanted to create some essays that have what people call "pop"—not "popular," but the "pop" of music—so I thought about the albums that I liked the most and thought about how a lot of them had strange musical interludes, and, you know, there were like three or four conventionally "popular" songs on those albums, but then there are often these songs that only people who really, really love the author liked. So, in that way, I thought how "How to Slowly Kill Yourself and Others" was kind of the "single"—it came out and went viral. "You Are the Second Person" was a soulful, bluesy, "plea" kind of song that a lot of people like. And the Michael Jackson, Bernie Mac, and Tupac [ones]—I have favorite albums that a lot of people like, but they only like a few songs on them, so I wanted to try to create that. But also within essays, I play a lot with repetition, so the "How To Slowly Kill Yourself and Others" essay is playing a lot with what they call a "dual repetition": the repetition of the line "I don't know what's wrong with me" and repetition of age ("three years older than"), and repetition is kind of what makes music, in some form or fashion (48). So that's the easiest answer for that. And my aunt—I got my aunt to write little introductions to one or two of the essays, and she's a gospel singer, she's super religious. The whole point was to get as many voices into one small book as possible, so you got her voice, you got my friend's voice in the middle in that echo" piece, you get my Uncle Jimmy's voice a little bit, you have my grandmother's voice throughout, [and] my mom's voice comes up every now and then. You got the voices of Pac, Mac [Tupac Shakur and Bernie Mac]. I just wanted to do a whole lot and make it seem like I wasn't trying to do much.

MB: You talk about Kanye's album *My Beautiful Dark Twisted Fantasy* (2010) in your essay collection. *How to Slowly Kill Yourself and Others in America* reminds me of that album, structurally. "All of the Lights" is the first track on Kanye's album, and that's one of the most popular songs, using some popular forms, and your first essay is the letter to your uncle, which is using this epistolary form that has become a literary tradition.

KL: See, you got it! You're right. Yeah, I was absolutely influenced by what he did. Musically, people say that might be his best album—we can argue about that.

MB: As someone who thinks about music and literature as interrelated, what do you think about Bob Dylan winning the Nobel Prize?

KL: What I have to say before anything else is, I'm not trying to shit on Dylan. I got nothing bad to say about the dude, but I don't know how much weight, intellectually, I can invest in an organization that has only given like six women over fifty years a Nobel Prize for literature. That to me is like, okay, if you only want to give six women a prize, that's your business, but to me that means you lack integrity. Not that you need to look to balance it—but that is absurd. So, because of that, I don't really care who they give it to. But when Morrison got it, I was like, of course she deserved it. So I'm happy when people who represent groups who usually don't get the things they deserve get things. The other thing is, I think the line between music and literature is really thin, but why does this white dude have to be the guy who bears this? The first time we do it, why does it have to be this white man, who also would tell you he borrowed so much style from Black performers, who I bet you were not even considered? So, one, there's so many other writers out there—women, white women, Black women, Indigenous women, all kinds of writers deserve it before him, absolutely. And I think, if you're going to make this big stand with music, I mean, there's Stevie Wonder, there's Aretha Franklin, there's Nina Simone, there's Bessie Smith—there's so many folks. And the argument is, "Oh, but Dylan's a poet," but who gets to decide what's lyrical or poetical in music? So I didn't get mad, I'm just like, "typical."

MB: In the essay collection [*How to Slowly Kill Yourself and Others in America*], you talk a lot about different artists that you listen to, and I've noticed that they span several decades. *Long Division*, of course, also spans several decades—1964, 1985, and 2013. Did your listening choices have anything to do with the different decades in which you were writing?

KL: Yeah, that's a great question. There's this woman named Halona King, and she's an independent local artist, and she does this song called "Monsters in the Night," and whenever I was writing the sections about Baize near the end of the book, when she starts to disappear, I was listening to that. And I was listening to Maxwell. Maxwell has a song called "Pretty Wings," and there's this falsetto part that is what I heard from not Baize but City when he realized that she was gone. But I didn't write that until I heard that part of the song. And then when I was writing the 1980s part, I listened to a lot of 1980s hip-hop, 1980s soul. I listened to a lot of the gospel music my grandmother used to play, a lot of Mahalia Jackson. I listened to some 2013 music just to get in the minds of City and LaVander Peeler because they're going back and forth with each other the way people do when they boast or when they're playing the dozens, so I listened to a lot of battle rap.

MB: Do you imagine Baize's rap music in *Long Division* to sound like any particular artist?

KL: I do. I mean, I know she sounds a bit like this kid that I tutored in Poughkeepsie. But she doesn't really sound like anybody famous. She's vulnerable like all children are. She uses her words and her responses to people, and really her adjectives, to defend herself. In my mind, her voice was just this young woman who I worked with.

MB: One of the things that really fascinates me about Baize is her relationship with YouTube. She has all these hits on YouTube, where she posts her raps, which suggests that even after she disappears, her music continues. Could you talk a little bit more about that? What is it that makes the role of digital archives intriguing to you?

KL: I try to mask my obsession with theory in my writing, but I like heavy theory, and performance theory is like chocolate to me—I love reading it. The thing about Baize is, we see her, we read her lyrics, we read her attempt to mediate herself when City gets her computer. So that's one way that she's going to live regardless—with words. And with YouTube, we have to think about how the physical body and physical death is . . . sort of important, but now everybody has access to keep themselves "alive." If you look at what Baize is doing on that computer, she's writing her life on that computer and then performing a particular kind of life on YouTube. Baize, to me, is the writer of *Long Division*, so there's also the mediation between all of the versions of *Long Division*. She cannot just write her life—she is a fully realized human being even though she's not treated that way, and she can imagine other lives. She can imagine 1984, she can imagine her family that she lost in Katrina, she can do all these things and put it in a book. Long story short, all I'm thinking about is performance, and her performance of self and her performance of dealing with trauma. For me, *Long Division*, the physical book, is this young Black Southern girl's desire to perform and imagine her trauma.

MB: It's interesting that the archive is mediated by technology in so many ways throughout this book. But it also seems important that in the end, the story, or the life being written, still depends on City sitting down with the blank pages and physically writing.

KL: Yeah, that's the heavy-handedness of the book. With all of these new mediums and stuff, I don't want people to forget the sentence. The sentences will always be there, and then the sentences for our behavior will always be there—the way we get sentenced as a result of things we should or shouldn't do. They'll always be there, and you can go back and read them. And, yes, the images and YouTube will always be there, too, but these sentences and the oral sentences shouldn't be forgotten.

MB: The "Can You Use This Word in the Sentence?" contest, to me, has uncomfortable—I mean that in a productive way—undertones of minstrel performance. I'm thinking about Eric Lott's book, *Love and Theft: Blackface Minstrelsy and the American Working Class* (2013), among others. Lott defines minstrelsy as a practice "in which men caricatured blacks for sport and profit" (3). In the case of the contest, the judges aren't doing the acting themselves, but they are building City into a caricature of sorts by giving him words with specific cultural connotations and controlling how far he can get in the contest. Were you thinking about the idea of minstrelsy when you wrote that scene?

KL: Absolutely, and I'm playing with Ellison's "Battle Royale" in *Invisible Man* (1952). But it's all about minstrelsy, it's all about Lott's understanding of minstrelsy and kind of a remix of the battle royale. I'm using the first-person narrator to look over at one kid who understands that, in this contest, he can't win. City ironically thinks he can win, and LaVander thought he could win, too, but when he realizes that he can't, it just breaks his heart.

MB: Do you think that LaVander's desire to be the "exceptional" African American is related to that sort of calculated minstrel performance? Is he playing into that, knowingly or unknowingly?

KL: I think he's playing into that, but he's also playing into this idea of representation. He believes, "If I perform really well then these white people will know that we can perform well." So there's an awareness, but there's also an expectation that however he acts can change these people. But when he realizes that there will be no changing—you're not an agent, you've been given a script—and when he realizes that they're letting him win for them, it just breaks him. And when City realizes that, it breaks him, too.

MB: This novel is also concerned with Hurricane Katrina. I think immediately of Jesmyn Ward and her novel *Salvage the Bones* (2011). In an interview, Ward said she was "disappointed with the way [Katrina] had retreated from national consciousness" (Hoover). How are you dealing with Katrina in your work?

KL: I lived in New York when Katrina happened, and it was terrible because I wasn't home. A lot of my family was really impacted and had to move and had to deal with a lot of death and destruction and all of that. You know, Baldwin writes about Bessie Smith . . . singing about the flood of 1928, and she's just like, "The water took my home, I don't live there no more." And for Baldwin, he thought, there's this acceptance of disaster . . . that shit happened, I don't have a home, but there's still forward movement, I still have to go forward with no home. So, for me, Katrina is a real thing in my book, but it's also reflecting on the fact that we're dealing with a country [that] is so maniacal in its abuse that it would do what it did to those kids on the stage. For a lot of Americans in the South, because that's where a lot of Black folk in the country live, you're dealing with what happened and what's happening with prison industrial complexes and Jim Crow and mass eviction. There's some way in which Katrina, a natural disaster, is just what we've been conditioned to deal with. Really, I'm trying to say: look, a flood can come and absolutely swallow a community, and nobody cares, for the most part. So if that can happen, you know what else can happen? Cats can fucking talk. Klan members can start dancing on YouTube. You can't tell me what's real or surreal when Americanness and Americans' relationships to our bodies is so surreal.

MB: Thinking further about relationships with our bodies, that scene at the end of *Long Division* where City is in the hole with somebody—we're not sure who it is—is such a physical experience for City and the reader. City is described as touching this person's features, but it's not until he lights the lighter that he actually knows who the person is. That particular scene to me was really evocative of what bodies can and can't tell us.

KL: With that scene, I'm torn because I don't want to, like, give it away. My next novel extends *Long Division*, sort of. I'll just say that embodiment is real, bodies are real. It's important for City at his most alone, his most isolated time. It's important for him to reach out and touch and feel and smell somebody there. But what I'm trying to say in this book is, imagination can embody. And I think reading is a form of embodiment. I think if I do my job as a writer, I can put some readers in that hole. I can't put every reader in that hole, but there's some readers who I know are in that hole.

MB: I have read a couple other interviews you've done, and you often get asked how biographical *Long Division* is. I'm actually more interested in how your experiences as an adult in the world have influenced the way you narrate City as a young Black boy in the South. Can you speak to that?

KL: That's a great question. My experiences as an adult impacted that book in a lot of ways. Primarily because, as an adult, I finally had the words to wrap around what I see. And what I see is—this is cliché, but—nobody's innocent. And that's not a bad thing, but complicity is just so real. That's why I wanted to start the first paragraph with the first narrator just saying he hates another boy. And then I wanted him to love that boy. And then I wanted the guy that he hates, who I wanted the reader to think was kind of a jerk, I wanted the reader to eventually feel for him. Even the white dude in the shed—I wanted the readers to in some ways feel for him. As an adult, you get older, and you see that everybody is abusive and gentle, and [there are] variations of both. That more than anything else came into the writing of that book. I didn't want to create any characters that were just completely disposable. I mean, some people read it and tell me they think the white characters are completely disposable, but I didn't want to do that.

MB: Speaking of your white characters, I also wanted to talk about Evan. What is his relationship to the book? What inspired you to write this Jewish character who is sort of passing as a Klan member? That's such a strong moment of performance, when Evan says, "No, no I'm not in the Klan," and Baize says, "Well, you're white and you're wearing a white sheet so . . ." (Laymon, *Long* 235).

KL: [*Laughs*] Right, right. You know, I had to do a lot of research for this book even though it probably didn't seem like it, and I interviewed this Jewish family on the coast of Mississippi. There were church bombings in the 1950s and 1960s, a lot of Black churches but also some synagogues, and I wanted to talk to some Jewish folks about how they felt like local terror affected their lives. And one of the stories I heard was that the Klan came to one of the Jewish families on the coast and told them that they had to terrorize this Black family during Freedom Summer. That's really where Evan came from. And I was thinking, what if the Klan came to Black ancestors of mine and were like, you have to go and blow up a synagogue, and you have to kill Jewish people, or we're going to kill you? It would never happen that way, but if it did, I kind of think my people, to survive, would be like, okay. I think most people would be like, okay, I want to survive. I'm not saying Jewish people were all involved in the Klan at all; a lot of Jewish people in Mississippi were really committed to fighting for their freedom and their abilities to have second choices and to help us fight. Historically, there's a relationship there. So I'm not at all saying Jewish folks were or are Klan members, but I'm saying that in this one family, that's what white Klan people have done. They've asked the family—a lot of them young boys—to do these things. So before we condemn Evan (and we can't really condemn Evan because he does fight back, he's just confused), [we have to think about that history]. The basis for that character came up from that interview.

MB: In *How to Slowly Kill Yourself and Others in America*, you have a fictional interview with political figures called "Reasonable Doubt and the Lost Presidential Debate of 2012." That essay drew me in some ways toward Chimamanda Ngozi Adichie's novel *Americanah* (2013). She has a scene where Obama wins the presidential election, and everyone reacts in an incredible way, and the narrator herself feels this strong sense of elation. I was comparing that scene to the scene that you write, about Obama winning and you not feeling elated but instead having the realization that the backlash is coming, that a step forward in one space necessitates a step back, or even violent retribution, in some other space.

KL: I think that's true. I think people were happy to have beaten white men because I think white men kind of dictate who becomes president. And even in that election, white people generally voted for McCain, voted for Romney. I forgot I wrote that. I talk about going downtown in Poughkeepsie after it happened, and people weren't celebrating down there.

MB: But they were celebrating on Vassar's campus?

KL: Oh yeah, I lived on campus at the time, and they were going off. One of my students said, "Congratulations!" And I was like, "Hmm, congratulations to you, too?" People definitely thought, I think, that American history was going to make a sharp turn. And maybe it turned, but it came back with a vengeance if it ever really left.

MB: When we talk about these violent histories, I wonder how we, as academics in these academic spaces, can work to push back against the violence. How can we take these spaces, that in some ways are isolated, or privileged, and use them as platforms to do better?

KL: Yeah, that's a big old question! And I don't have the answer. But on one level, I think we're perfectly situated. Because our jobs, literally, are to educate, and [there are] so many different kinds of academics—people at community colleges, Harvard, state colleges, historically black colleges and universities—and different positionalities—able-bodied folk, trans folk, women. So whatever I'm about to say is not a collective for everybody. But one thing I think is that we have to realize that wherever we are in the nation, and at our college/university, power and abuses of power are working the same way even if it's at a different frequency. I can bet, for example, that the people on the board of trustees of this institution have never taken a course on gender studies, critical race studies, [disability] studies. So what does it mean that in this weird academic institution, the people who run the whole school are uneducated? Miseducated? That means that the policies they put forth are going to be kind of suspect. So I think the first thing we can do is put pressure on our departments, our areas, and ultimately our institutions to show that they really value education by making the presidents, administrators, board of trustees, and faculty [commit to education around] issues of sexuality, gender, race, power. And not just for one course—they need a sustained education. As academics we can do what we do best, which is describe and analyze, but sometimes we need to put our bodies in the way. We need to say, "No, we want answers, meaning, we want these people, here, to be treated as fairly as the group of people here." I don't think we should let these jobs stop us from actually doing what we say we care about.

MB: I'm interested in the way gender operates in your novel and stories. In the essay "Hip Hop Stole My Southern Black Boy," you talk about how hip-hop has yet to love and nourish Black girls in the way that it has nourished you and your friends, in your personal experience. You have these really strong Black girls in *Long Division*, and I'm wondering how you built those characters. Are they based on women in your life? And then, as an extension of that question, what does hip-hop need to do to love Black girls? What does society need to do?

KL: I guess I'm saying in that hip-hop essay that the problems that hip-hop has are just the problem that the country has! You know, when Obama did the My Brother's Keeper initiative, to help Black boys across the country, a number of us organized and fought back and said, "Okay, but if you're just teaching boys that they have to be stronger men, that's terrible." And secondly, you need to look at the data that says Black girls particularly are being invisibilized and struggling and being targeted. So a bunch of us organized, did letter writing, strategized. We went to the White House to talk to My Brother's Keeper architects, and what they literally told us was, "Black girls can wait." And you know, we were people who had done our work and we were saying, "Black girls cannot wait." You can't look at the same data that you're looking at for Black boys. And Black girls have to deal with Black boys and Black men hurting them. So I'm saying the White House's response was kind of like, "We have to deal with the boys right now." And as for hip-hop—that has been hip-hop's response, too. So my critique of hip-hop isn't isolated; I think it's happening on a larger scale. But unless we radically reform education from "K" through "life," I don't think you're going to get music that is really attending to the lack of love or the love that vulnerable groups need. So, thankfully, there are a lot of MCs that are women and trans, that are doing their own work. But, you know, we also have to be careful not to put folks on pedestals. They need work, too. They need to think about power and socioeconomics and ableism. So I try not to come down hard on hip-hop too much. The thing that hip-hop has done is put class stratification in our face in a way that most popular forms of entertainment haven't. There's always a conversation about what the complete lack of economic mobility can do for you socially, what new money can do for you socially. That's something that you see in hip-hop more than other genres. But there aren't enough songs that talk about how poverty impacts Black girls and women in different ways than white boys and men.

MB: You said that your next book is a memoir. Or rather you said it's being marketed as a memoir, which is an interesting way to describe it.

KL: Yeah. I mean, I always try to do stuff that I haven't seen done before. It's not a letter to my mother, it's a memoir to my mother and some other people. Really, it's not even a memoir, but that's what they market it as because that's what people buy—people buy memoirs.

MB: How is that writing process different? You have a diverse body of work, with the memoir and novels and essays. How are those processes different as a writer?

KL: Oh man! There's a lot of smart things I could say, but [the memoir is] just the hardest thing I've ever done. I think about *Long Division*, *How to Slowly Kill Yourself and Others in America*, and the memoir [*Heavy: An American Memoir* (2018)] as a series of books that should be read together. The essay book [*How to Slowly Kill Yourself and Others in America*] ends with a letter to my mom, where I'm saying, "I understand." And then this book is just me trying not to pass anymore as the son she thinks I am; I'm trying to show her some of what I experienced and what I saw her do, but I'm also trying to show stuff that she might have seen that the reader will understand I might not have. It's tough because some of this is my momma's business, her personal life. She doesn't like any of my writing because she thinks I reveal too much about me, and she thinks other people could use that to hurt me. And this—I'm putting some of her stuff out there. It's hard.

MB: I loved reading about the process of getting *Long Division* published. In your talk last night, you mentioned that it was almost about "two white girls from Upstate New York." You also said you envisioned it as "an American race novel." I was wondering if you could speak to what that means, exactly. Is it writing in a particular tradition or maybe forging a new tradition? Has what defines "an American race novel" changed over time?

KL: I think it is a new tradition. I think a lot of younger people and some older people have taught us that when we're talking about race, we also have to talk about geography and orientation and gender, so the race novel of 2016 hopefully has different rules than *Invisible Man*, than the race novel of 1930-something. Intersectionality now is a word—everybody talks about it, and it's real. I think real thoughtful race books are really thoughtful about the things that intersect with race. Just like real thoughtful geography books are thoughtful about the things that intersect with traditional geography. And I think I did it, honestly. I revised that book a lot. I revise it still. And Lord knows it's not perfect, but the hardest stuff I wanted to do, I did, and I feel good that I can say that.

MB: Is science fiction influential for you? You have the time travel plot in *Long Division*, and you even reference Voltron.

KL: My real friends would say I'm definitely not a science fiction person. But Voltron was a cartoon, he comes together with four or five different parts. I was into how Voltron was made up of different parts, and then he came together to fight whoever. We're all held together with different parts. Like I'm looking at you now, and you're doing graduate school, but you're also like, "I'm a runner," and you're running and nobody sees the graduate student. We're all different kinds of people who come together.

MB: About the time-travel plot, it's interesting to me to think that we can travel through time and rewrite history, for better or for worse. But what's especially compelling to me about the time-travel plot is the realization that these conflicts in the novel—even though they take place in different years—could have been put in any of the three settings, and they would have still been realistic. The narratives of oppression, coming-of-age, performance, family struggles—these transcend time, in a way. Is that something you were cognizant of as you were developing the novel?

KL: Sure. A lot has changed, but the way we abuse kids, the way we abuse groups—it doesn't change that much. Obviously, there's no YouTube in the 1980s, so that contest and the thing going viral is specific. You [couldn't] mediate yourself the same way in the 1980s as you can now. But you can still terrorize particular bodies now. And the scary part is, we're obsessed with progress, so we always want to believe that whatever messed-up thing happened yesterday can't happen today. But we never really talk about what really happened yesterday. If you don't deal with what happened yesterday, who you were yesterday, you're never going to really transform, ever. You can't. It's impossible to get to B if you haven't thought about how A looks, smells, tastes, all that kind of stuff.

MB: Before we go, I want to ask about the new novel. You said it's an extension of *Long Division*. Is it an extension story-wise? Or idea-wise?

KL: Kind of idea-wise.

MB: Can I ask who's in it?

KL: Baize is in it. She's grown-up though. I don't have kids or anything, so I feel like I became happily connected to some of those characters and her especially. I like her a lot.

MB: I'm looking forward to it. Thank you so much for your time today.

The People of Jackson Are Ready: Chokwe Antar Lumumba in Conversation with Kiese Laymon

Kiese Laymon / 2019

From *Southern Cultures*, 2019. Reprinted with permission.[1]

Kiese Laymon: Yo, man. It's so good to talk to you, fam. I don't even know how to ask somebody as busy as you how you doing. Are you less busy in the summer, or does it ramp up?

Chokwe Antar Lumumba: It's no season for it, man. It's an all-year-round thing. But I'm good, I'm enjoying it. I enjoy what I do. A lot of challenges, but I look forward to them, bro.

KL: One of my questions though, brother, I've said this to you publicly. I've told a lot of other people privately. I think that you and the movement have made a lot of people look at Jackson in ways they hadn't looked at Jackson before. I think the notion of Jackson being the most progressive, radical city in the world, in the country, is something that has drawn folks. My first question is: Do you feel like in order to be the most radical city in the country, that you have to be the most radical mayor in the country? Is there a correlation between those two?

CAL: I think how I'm viewed, in terms of how radical I am, is for someone else's interpretation. What I would say is, this movement really is a people's movement. As my father [Chokwe Lumumba, mayor of Jackson, 2013–2014] would say, "A selection of our leadership represents the readiness of the people." It means that the people of Jackson are ready for something. They're very consciously going after something that is pushing the envelope. That is forcing us to look inward, forcing us to address our contradiction, forcing us to not only look at our society in our city in terms of how it provides dignity to people, how it addresses issues of self-determination and people's ability to dictate their lives, but also how it delves into me as a man—how I live in a patriarchal, sexist society. Yesterday we were labeled the first equal-pay-committed destination because we think that it is indicative of the values we have as a community and the ordinance we passed is a moral document. It says to my children—it says to my little girls that we can no longer accept that you get paid less through the course of your life for the same, if not better, work that a man does. So how do we begin to leverage our power so that we can start building institutions that we own as a community? Institutions [where] the mission of them is to serve the community, and they don't go anywhere unless the community says so. I certainly support Black business. I certainly think in an 85-percent Black city, it's not even a matter of race. It's a matter of economics. If 85 percent of your population is left-handed, then you need some left-handed jobs.

KL: That's right.

CAL: Even beyond that, a Black business is like any other business in a capitalist society, in exploit markets. Once it's taken all that it can from the market that gave birth to it, it might just leave and vacate the community that gave rise to it and look for higher returns. That's why cooperative enterprise, worker-owned cooperatives—where people can not only dictate their labor, but dictate what the fruits of their labor will be—enables us to have a holistic view of how we fill our voids and at the same time take better care of one another.

KL: I love that, man. One of the things that you say. . . . It's strange. I'm older than you, but your father was like an older brother to my father and to my mother. My father was in the Republic of New Afrika [a Black nationalist organization and Black separatist movement founded in 1968]. I think a lot about how—again, I'm a bit older than you, but we were still raised, I think, with this notion of Black race-men. One of the things you said about equity really made me think about whether or not you think there is an importance in having formal representation be equitable too. When you were gracious enough to make that proclamation [to honor my writing], and I came down and I looked at the city council, there was part of me that was shocked at how many men were on that city council when I know how many women really comprised the movement. That is not at all taking shots at anybody who is on the council. I'm just thinking about the way formal representation works in the minds of people who want to see an equitable—particularly a gender-equitable—city, state, world. Can you talk a bit about whether or not formal representation has a role in gender equity when it comes to a city like Jackson?

CAL: Absolutely, absolutely. I think that oppression is a very intricate process, it's deep. You can be oppressed by people who don't look like you, who don't share similar characteristics to you, and you can be oppressed by people who look just like you and fall into whatever category of connection that you have with them. The issue is, I do believe, just as with the fight in the Reconstruction Era, where black folks in Mississippi. . . . See, Mississippi didn't just now come to the forefront, trying to push progressive ideas. After slavery, it was in Mississippi that the first public school system was adopted. It was in Mississippi that Black folks started to think about their own economic security. It was in Mississippi that Black people . . . who had the right to vote immediately after slavery, who, instead of doing what the Union Soldiers and Union Representatives expected them to do, in electing them, did what anyone would do and elected themselves.

KL: Right, right.

CAL: That same principle is one worth considering for women, right? Very few people are going to support the aims and concerns of women like women, right? We have to be honest in that sometimes those who submit to that oppression of women most consistently are women. I've seen women carry some of the most negative impressions of other women and not really have a progressive view of themselves. I think that all those things have to be dealt with. We have to challenge that and be introspective at the same time.

KL: All right. I love that, bro. So, this is one of my biggest questions. This is probably a question I should ask you when we're not recording. We can deal with this question or not. I have friends, as you do, in all these cities that are no doubt gentrified. A lot of the Black leadership of these cities. . . . The aim for a lot of Black leadership seems to be gentrification. Sometimes when I'm talking to my friends, I'm like, "I feel you all, I see what all is happening, but what's going on in Jackson is something different." Sometimes when I'm just with my people, I'm like, "Jackson seems gentrification-proof." Because we both know people whose aim for Jackson is really a particular kind of gentrification. So I'm interested in not just your assessment of where we are in Jackson, but in terms of vision. Do you actually, and the leadership team and the movement particularly, need and want more progressive white folk to move into the city? And if so, how do we want Jackson to be different than what we see happening in New Orleans, or parts of Birmingham, or Little Rock? I don't know if that's a question you can actually answer, but I'm interested in what your thoughts are.

CAL: No, I don't have a problem with answering that question. Well, first and foremost, we want a city which is open and welcoming to anybody who is of goodwill and sincerity, that wants to join. But we are very openly and proudly . . . I oppose the idea of gentrification. I think gentrification is a war against people. Where it moves people from one state of misery to. . . . So we have to envision a system or a city that looks at building opportunity for people around there. When I'm thinking about building a better Jackson, it's not just about great edifices, nice new buildings, better roads. It's about building a city for the souls that reside in the city, right?

KL: Right, right.

CAL: It's about honoring their legacy and not restricting anyone else's enjoyment of that, but understanding that effort to change is not to be at the detriment of someone else, right? Ultimately, when people find themselves fearful of change, it's not really change that they're afraid of. It's loss. If we can get rid of this notion of loss, [and remember the value of] improving someone else's conditions, being considerate of all sectors of Jackson, [then we can understand] that we can't build islands of wealth surrounded by a sea of poverty. We have to build the narrative around if that happens, if someone leaves, if someone is not able to access their greatest potential in a certain part of the city, then the burden is shifted to all parts of the city, right? Greater tax burden. We don't live in the *Hunger Games* bubble, right? When crime takes place, everyone is potentially impacted by that crime. We have to understand we have a shared destiny. We have to have a shared vision and shared prosperity.

KL: I love that, bro. Just one and a half more questions. The other question I have is connected to that. . . . Can police forces actually be progressive, radical sites of liberation? If they cannot, what, then, is a movement's job? What responsibility do the people have to move a police force in a city like Jackson?

CAL: Yeah. The honest answer to that is in this country we need a complete reconstruction of our criminal justice system. We don't need reform. We need to break it down and start over again. And I say that because we've allowed this to be a predominant portion of our economy. That means we have an overreliance on incarceration of Black bodies. This is a country that has taken advantage of bodies, underserved and underrepresented bodies. Because of that, what you see now is more police than you've ever seen in our world. You see our city police, your county police, your state police, your federal police, your secret police, your secret police who watch the secret police, right?

KL: Right.

CAL: We say that crime doesn't pay. You also have your judges, your lawyers. You have all of those people whose livelihoods is connected to our criminal justice system. So what does that require? That requires an overincarceration of our world and overincarceration of our society. I think that we're falling into this habit of insanity, where you continue to do the same things over and over again and expect a different result.

If overpolicing our society led to safer communities then we would have the safest communities on the planet, but we have more police than any other country in the world and we have more crime than any other country in the world. We have to understand that the issue of policing is not exclusive to the issue of safety, to the issue of reducing crime. Now, with that being said, Jackson certainly has his challenges with its police department. Many of those things are reflected in what is in occupational culture that has to be changed. Do I believe Jackson mirrors some of the more negative trends around the country? Maybe not entirely. I don't think that entirely because a lot of people who make up our police department look like those people they're policing.

KL: Right.

CAL: So they understand this dynamic of the relationship between Black community and police. Although it does not necessarily prevent the occasion of unfortunate circumstances taking place. Because I think that we have a population that our police force can relate to slightly differently. I think there's an opportunity to build a better relationship. Does it exist yet? No, it doesn't. It doesn't exist as we would have [liked] for it to exist, but that's why we believe that we have to really support community sensitivity programs. We're trying to push a citizen's review board that has subpoena power. What we had was an officer ID task force. We put the task force—made up of both communities, overwhelmingly majority community and some officers—so they can talk about the impact of their safety and how it felt. What we saw come out of that process, when we had a police department and all of those officers that were initially on that task force, which were adamantly opposed to their ID being released after an officer-involved shooting. They learned from the community, and they unanimously voted together in order to release within a seventy-two-hour period. They unanimously entered into that after a process of really being able to imagine the perspectives of one another. I think that that is promising. It is far from declaring victory, but it is a minor success that we have to continue to move forward with.

KL: Man. Thank you for that, bro. Last question is . . . I think sometimes we focus on the word *good* or *bad*. Both of us are people who I think appreciate language. I think "good" or "bad" just don't have enough texture. If we could talk about just terror and joy as two separate things—I'm interested in what has been the most unexpected joyful experience as mayor of Jackson. Also, I'm wondering if you could talk about, if you feel comfortable, what has been the most terrifying. Could you talk about that just as briefly or as fully as you want?

CAL: Being entrusted with this responsibility. Constantly being approached by my elders, being approached by different people in the city and just speaking to their gratitude for the efforts that we're trying to make is rewarding. It gives me energy. I love people, I really do. People tell you, when there's a parade in the city, I literally get out there and try to shake every hand, enjoy conversations, and talk to people. I even enjoy when people try to give me advice because I think it sharpens me. The people are honestly the most joyful thing to me. We just recently started these pop-up visits in the community with our directors, where we're going to different communities, and we literally put all the directors on a bus. So that it's not just a process of making decisions from an office for people that you've never met, property and area that you've never seen. You get an opportunity to be face-to-face with people and lay your eyes on the problem and challenges they see. We had a process where we knocked on 60,000 doors, talked to people. That has been the greatest joy. Just the interaction with people, the support, and engagement of people. We've been able to do some amazing things. One, save the school district. Take a city that had a $6 million deficit when we came into office and turn it into a $12 million surplus. Take city employees off of furlough. We give them a small 2 percent raise, which was really more of a pledge of where we're headed and what we're going to do for people who haven't received a raise in over a decade, to ensure that we have a living wage in our city. All of those things give me energy, give me life, are exciting to me. I guess the terror is this city has been taken advantage of. When I see people who have extremely high water bills because of exploitative contracts that were for political favors. I see elderly ladies and elderly men come up to city hall and showing me that they got $3,000, $5,000 water bills that they have no way of paying and the state doesn't allow for us to forgive those debts. We're trying to figure out how we make it feasible for them to not cut off their water and take care of them, as the city is cash strapped. That is a horrific sight, but at the same time, I'm strange in that I like challenges, brother. I really do. I like challenges. It doesn't mean that I feel good throughout the challenge. There are definitely days where I'm shaking my head. I may even curse, you know?

KL: Right.

CAL: And pace a bit, trying to figure it out. But, at the same time, the joy of solving it is one that enables us to embrace new challenges. There are moments of, "Wow, this is a really big mountain ahead of us." We have to figure out how we go around it or, like Hannibal, how we just run the troops up the mountain.

Note

1. Despite Mayor Chokwe Lumumba's indictment in November 2024 on bribery charges, he has maintained his innocence and will have his day in court in July 2026. These allegations do not negate Lumumba's vision for the city of Jackson at the time that Laymon interviewed him in 2019.

Interview with Scott Peters for the Kenan Institute for Ethics at Duke University

Scott Peters / 2020

From Duke University's Ethics of Now Series, https://kenan.ethics.duke.edu/a-conversation-with-kiese-laymon, March 17, 2020. Reprinted with permission.

Scott Peters: What is your primary objective as an author?

Kiese Laymon: My primary objective in my work is to discover things I don't understand, discover different ways into things I do understand. The secondary objective I have is to communicate that discovery to people with some sort of profundity. Ultimately, I'm also interested in innovation. I want people to feel like they are reading something they maybe never read before, but they need it. I think it's hard to be innovative and soulful. I think innovation and soulfulness sort of kind of run counter to one another, so I want to be innovative, and I want to be discoverable, but I also want to be . . . I want to hit people in the chest.

SP: Does that discovery happen in your planning process or does that happen as you're writing?

KL: Writing is my planning process. I'm a rabid reviser, I'm one of those people. My first fifteen drafts are terrible, but they're useful to me because they get me to places I couldn't have gotten to without them. I know some people who do a lot of writing and revision in their head before they write. I know brilliant writers who do that. I kind of have to think as I write as opposed to mulling it over in my head. When I'm in a project I'm using my phone, I'm typing, I'm using pad and pencil, so the writing process is the discovery process for me.

SP: How did you decide on the memoir format for *Heavy*?

KL: I've written a book called *Long Division*; I've written a book of essays called *How to Slowly Kill Yourself and Others in America*. I think when I was writing those two books, I was trying to write through what I was writing through in *Heavy*, I just didn't have the skill, I did not have the will. I was a judge for the National Book Award and I just had to read seven-hundred nonfiction books, most of which were memoirs. At that point I was like, "Oh wow, this is a form that consumers tend to like because they feel like it's a tell-all." But I think a lot of times memoirs are not artistically rendered. I think some people call a memoir a memoir, but really those memoirs are autobiographies, meaning that people are like, "I'm going to tell you about where I was born, what my mother did." And I just wanted to use a lot of my fictive tools, my essayistic tools, to create a memoir piece of art as opposed to a tell-all.

And so, for me, that's what I really wanted to do. I like reading memoirs, but I think a lot of times memoirists forget the importance of the artistry of it. That's one of the reasons I wrote it to my mom, because I hadn't seen any memoirs do that at the time. The name of the book is *Heavy*, letting people know that every chapter and almost every word in that book should be read at least three different ways. I think that word plays with misdirection in a way that I'm really interested in. So I just wanted to do a little bit more artful stuff that you might see in poetry or nonfiction in a memoir form, where sometimes people, again, read as being straightforward autobiography. Which I don't think it is. I don't think it should be.

SP: There's a struggle in *Heavy* over whose stories get to be remembered. Can you talk about memory and the role that it plays in the book and even further, how does that play in today's political landscape?

KL: I'll go with the first part. So the first part is that when I first started doing this I was like, "I'm trying to find the truth," you know? But I think, as most of us know, the truth is so elusive, right? I just spent forty-five minutes talking to some brilliant students, and I think if they all were to write truthfully about what happened, hopefully we would get, however many kids were in there, twelve different renderings of that truth, right? Which means that there cannot be an essential truth. But I think we do know when we're trying to avoid a truth. I'm more interested in honesty than truth, and the way sometimes we know we are attempting to be dishonest. And politically, I wish I could say that Trump started this, I mean, just sick desire to never look back and never regret what one has done poorly or to harm people. I wish that I could say that.

But Trump took it to another level, right? Trump never takes responsibility, but most of our American Presidents don't take responsibility for things they've done wrong. And as an educator, I just don't know how you get better if you don't revise. Revision is rooted in, "I'm going to look back at what I did, see the holes in it, see the gaps in it, accept the gaps, articulate the gaps, so the gaps are no longer gaps. Or so readers can see that I am a fractured person." I think we'd be in a better place if we wanted to elect people who were woefully looking backward at mistakes. I don't think we want to do that. I actually think political workers get punished for doing it, so I get why they don't do it, but I think we need that. I still think we look to the presidency for some sort of leadership, and I think we look to politicians for some sort of leadership, and I think we need, and I sound like my grandma, but I think we need rhetorical leadership as much as we need moral leadership, and you can't have either if you don't ask, "What do you most regret in your political life? What have you contributed to most that has harmed people?" And those are the questions I think that matter most, not as gotcha moments, but so these people won't repeat these things that they've done. And nobody asks that question of them, so they never answer that question, and that's scary. It's really frightening to be led by groups of people who we don't even want to ask to honestly assess themselves and do better. Since I'm not a politician, I want to use the page to do some of that work, so in my real life I can be a lot less harmful, a lot more rooted in tender relationships than con relationships, but if you're not willing to look back and accept and admit your faults and mistakes, I mean I'm not sure what we're doing. It's really scary to me where we are. But we didn't just get here, that's what I have to keep telling myself. Trump didn't invent cowardice. He perfected it, but he didn't invent it. Yeah.

I played sports in high school, I played basketball and football in college, and I have lots of faults, but I was never one of those dudes where if I knocked the ball out in basketball, I wasn't going to be like, "It didn't go off me," which is what most people do, right? They lie, because they just want to win. I think that desire to just win when you're talking about something like the quality of people's lives, the quantity of people who get to share in the spoils of this country, I think that's scary. I think we got to get beyond winning. Winning can't be the end. I mean, that's where we are, people just want to win at all costs. I don't think anything good comes to us as a society or world, but definitely not vulnerable, vulnerable people who don't have a pot to piss in, who don't have adequate insurance. Just trying to win doesn't really help those folks at all. Just trying to win doesn't help people that are just trying to eat or just trying to fucking go get a shot that they can afford for their children, or people who work. I don't know who cleans this building, but in my institution, people who clean buildings don't get living wages at all, and just trying to win is not helping the people who deserve to be helped most. I hope we get beyond this idea of just trying to win.

And the sad thing is that one way you win now, if you're a particular kind of person, is that you tell people that these vulnerable people are leeches, right? You tell people that the vulnerable people who actually don't have much, and I don't care if those people are undocumented folks, if they're Black people working on the Delta, if you make certain Americans believe that those people are asking for more than they deserve, that's a way to win, that's scary. And that to me has little to do with the presidential candidate, it has everything to do with often who we are as people, and definitely as Americans. It's not a sport, it's not a sport. I'm not out there rooting for my team. Because if you root for your team the way I think most of us know how to be fans, we're going to clap for calls that are categorically wrong. But the only reason we think they're wrong calls is if they go against us. And growing up where I grew up, where lots of people purport to be Christian, it runs counter to every kind of Christianity you could ever imagine.

My grandmother is, I think, the most die-hard radical Christian I've ever met, and she's not about winning, she's about reckoning. She's not about just trying to win, she's just about, "We got to reckon, and we got to do right by the least of these. Do right by the folks who have been done the most wrong to." That's my opinion. I mean, I don't get on the soapbox much, but you all kind of asked me to.

SP: How should universities (like Duke) reckon with Black suffering and embrace Black abundance?

KL: Presidents, boards of trustees, tenured faculty members, among others, first of all have to get together and assess the wrong, the harm the institutions have invested in that has led to an abundance of financial whatever. Right? We have to be honest about how these institutions got their wealth. And then once we're honest, and I think it's hard to be honest about that, I think once we're honest about that we have to talk about whether or not we have the will to repair that theft. I think that conversation might lead to people being like, "No, we don't have the will." But at least have on the record that all these people who are the power of these institutions have looked honestly and assessed and been like, "You know what, we don't have the will to do right by the folks who have made so many parts of these institutions and were never treated fairly."

And then I think any educational institution that's run by a board of trustees that doesn't have robust education as part of what the board of trustees' mission is, is a suspect institution. You can't call yourself an educational institution and then you don't [have] a requisite for the board of trustees to read any book. They don't have to read books by faculty, they don't have to read the newest nonfiction out, they have to go and make these decisions. I just question ultimately how much we value education when we don't make our most powerful people invest in education. I'm not talking about book clubs, I'm talking about sustained investment in education. Ultimately, I think what that does is it models a kind of radical sharing that we would say we want all of our students to have. We want our students to be educationally robust, we want our students to be abundant. We say we want them to be really good at creating and sharing, but I don't think we give them a model for that. And thankfully they come to things on their own, they push these institutions to do incremental changes, but it would be great if we gave them a model for actual radical sharing of resources, and/or a model of talking about why we don't have the will to do right. And that's not something I see in any institution actually. I mean, Georgetown is trying to do some of this stuff, but I don't see that anywhere else.

SP: You mentioned you wrote *Heavy* for your mother. What is it like having other people read this raw, almost private work?

KL: Honestly when I wrote it, there's so much that is taken out, and that I just hope people see and feel in the subtext of the book. But writing a book and putting a book out was hard, but it wasn't nearly as hard as going across the country talking to people who have read the book. I don't know about most writers, but I didn't think people were going to read the book. I didn't think I was going to win the Carnegie and *Los Angeles Times* Award, and all these other awards. And since that, I go into some places with people who have seen my insides before I even know how they are on the outside. What that often means is they want me to know about their insides, and they want me to tell them what they should do. And because I'm from Mississippi, my inclination is to try to help—but I'm not trained to do that. I'm not trying to be like, "Woe is me." But it makes it harder in a way that I didn't anticipate. I didn't anticipate hearing the stories that I hear from people everywhere I go and having to go to sleep with those stories in weird hotel rooms.

SP: That's a lot of weight to carry. All of a sudden people assume they have this personal relationship with you because they read your life?

KL: They think because you wrote it, you've reckoned—you're solid now. A lot of times people think because it's a product that you must be okay.

Again, it's hard to complain about this, but I'm only answering the question. Yeah, we're human beings, and human beings, particularly American human beings, the human beings I know the best, we're carrying a lot of stuff. Stuff we've done to people, stuff that's been done to us. Sometimes when you see people who appear to be trying to talk about that, it makes you think you want to talk to those people about what you've done. I have parents sometimes that want to talk to me about surviving sexual abuse, but also sexually abusing a child.

That's above my pay grade, you know what I'm saying? I don't know how to talk to a parent, but I know how to listen. Or what happens often in cisgender men who appear to be in really great shape will come and talk to me about their eating disorders, and how close to death they've been. And Lord knows, lots, and lots, and lots, and lots, and lots of women have come to talk to me about their relationships with sexual assault. Sometimes I just wish people could also look at the parts of the book that I think are about beauty and wonder and the awesomeness of language. But I think that when you write a book this way also because of the way we're taught to read memoirs, it's harder to talk about the joyful stuff than it is to talk about the super painful things.

SP: Why do you think people latch onto the painful things so willingly? And why don't you think people talk more about their issues?

KL: I think we latch on to what sounds familiar to our heart, but also when it appears that someone else has done work we also want to do some. We are fucked-up people. And I say that gleefully, we are fucked-up people who have the ability to talk about and work through that shit for ourselves, for the children coming after us, sometimes for our parents who definitely did not have the language to talk about a lot of the things that they were suffering with. And so, when people see a model of someone attempting to do that, there can be an attraction. But also, sometimes people just want answers. The most traumatic things that brought this book into the world are not textually in the book—they're subtextually in the book. The sexually violent relationships, familiar relationships that brought this book into the world for example, are not explicitly written about, but they're there. The concrete ways I have failed in my students and succeeded in loving them are not in that book. They're in the subtext of the book. I think sometimes, and this is maybe a little bit too artsy or literary, but sometimes I feel like people, without even having the language, can feel subtext. And I think when you create a piece of art with a lot of subtext, people just want to get closer to it. Definitely when I'm going across the country, people are like, "I feel like something else is happening in this paragraph. Could you tell me?" And I have to be like, "No. No, I told you what I want to tell you." And I told you a lot. You know way more about me than I know about you.

People will ask anything. People will be like, "Did your mom sexually assault you? What did she do to your body?" Literally, that's a common question for people who read the book, who have read *Heavy*. "Can you tell me what she did and when she did it? What time of day? Because I had similar experiences." Well, you can talk to me about those experiences if you want to, but I have given you what I'm going to give you about that. And I think I've given you a lot, but it's not a tell-all. I can't be doing the tell-all thing that a lot of people want. I think people just forget sometimes that it's the artful rendering of experience. It's the artful attempt to reckon. Art-full, right? Like artificial, right? It's art. I think people just want to see it as being real. I get it, because I'm trying to make them see it as real. You write a book like this, people just think they have access to every part of you, you know? "How come you ain't married? How come you don't have no kids? Have you tried?" "What the fuck? Damn."

I love conversations, but those kinds of conversations where people just want a catalog of more harmful shit, I'm not interested in that. I can't. But when I first went out on the road, and this is sort of interesting—I'm from Mississippi, I think our predispositions are really kind, meaning that if you buy my book, in my heart I think I owe you. That's what I feel. Even though you're buying it partially because I gave you so much, but there's a part of me that feels like if you buy the book that I'm responsible to tell you whatever you want. But I had to get away from that, because that wasn't healthy for me. But at first, any question people asked, I tried to give them the honest answer, which was not a good idea for lots of reasons.

SP: What's the relationship between masculinity and vulnerability in your writing?

KL: The easy answer is masculine-presenting people in this country are not taught to talk honestly about vulnerability, about the way we've been harmed, about the intricacies of how we harm. I think all of that's true. But I also wanted to talk about in that book, the ways that when I was young and didn't have the language. I don't even know if I ever used the word harm as a kid. Definitely didn't use the word white supremacy as a kid, had no idea what patriarchy meant. But I knew my friends and I loved each other, and I knew we couldn't wait to find excuses to hug. We loved to hug each other. Sports, I mean sports is not homosocial, it is homoerotic. And I'm not saying people want to fuck their teammates, but I'm saying I loved hugging my teammates, but that was one of the only times we could hug. I loved my boy telling me, "Man, I love you." But it was only on the sports field.

But I'm also trying to say, it's not like we weren't intimate. It's not like we weren't expressing intimacy. We were allowing masculinity in a lot of ways to prohibit us from going deeper. But I saw my friends cry a lot, and I saw my friends ridicule my other friends who were boys for falling in love. Like, "Man, you falling in love." That was the worst thing you could do was fall in love. "Where Derek at?" "Man, he fell in love." Anyway, I'm trying to do two things. One, be like, "Yes, we need to be better." But two, I just think we did show love, and care, and vulnerability to each other. And as Black boys particularly, became Black men, I think it's important to not act like that was completely absent. It was there, but we never talked about it. I never talked to my friends about how good it felt sometimes to just hug them. How good it felt to just spend the night at their houses. We didn't talk about that stuff, but we know it felt good. We know that sustained us.

SP: Were there parts of this story that didn't make it in the final version of *Heavy* that you're open to share?

KL: All throughout *Heavy* I use white space. There will be text, and then sometimes there'll be a sort of potentially provocative sentence, then there'll be a gap, and then there will be a sentence to start another section. An example of that is in the section where I talk about my mother's boyfriend. She picked me up from my friend's house, she was in the driver's seat, I was in the passenger seat. She wouldn't turn toward me. She finally turned to me, I saw that her eye was bleeding. She didn't have to tell me what happened, I knew that the guy she was with had beat her up. And when we get to the house I talk about going to get the gun, give a little bit more description, and then I say. . . . He comes over to the house that night while she's asleep and I say, "I tried to kill the radical Black man from Mississippi that night," because that's what he called himself. There's a gap. In real life, right? In real life I got the gun and I literally tried to kill. It reads metaphoric, right? "I tried to kill somebody." It doesn't read as if I had a gun, tried to shoot him. It just reads, "Oh, maybe he tried to fight him." I don't think that the concrete details of what actually happened in there are going to serve me, him, or my momma, so I took it out. But there are also lots of other examples that just weren't my stories to tell at all that have to do with my grandmother's romantic relationships. I took that out of the book, didn't need to tell those stories. Students who talked to me a lot about all kinds of stuff, I took all of that out of the book and then just summarized it in a paragraph talking about the ways that I failed my students but also wanted to be there for them in every way. But I failed. I took that out completely because that's not mine to tell. There's a ton of stuff that I just took out for art. Part of it is because it wasn't mine to tell, but also it was because I had an idea of how I wanted the art to move. I think sometimes, if I did some of what I just said, it would've bogged the art down and it would've appeared to be a little bit more salacious than I wanted it to be.

I tell my students the most important writing I did for *Heavy*, nobody ever saw. My momma saw. But other than my momma, nobody ever saw that, nobody ever will see it. But I needed to write it to get to other parts of the book, but also I needed to write it to get to other projects that I'm doing now. Some of that stuff might come up fictively in something else. I just believe everything we write we might be able to use somewhere else, so that makes me cool with taking out stuff. Whereas when I was a younger writer I was like, "Oh, if I delete it it's gone." That's why a lot of times the stuff I wrote as a young person was just terrible, because I was like, "I'm only going to write one book, and I got to put everything in there." My graduate thesis was seven-hundred pages of bullshit, because . . . I mean, it wasn't bullshit, but it was seven-hundred pages that didn't cohere because I literally did not ever think I would get a chance to do a second book. And I just think you have to trust, even if it's not true, you got to trust that you'll get a chance to do a second project, because you can overwhelm a first project with all that mess.

SP: What books are on your bedside table?

KL: Again, I was a National Book Award judge this year, so we had to read seven-hundred books. I gave away two hundred or so of them, but I got like five-hundred books all on my table, all on my counters in my kitchen. But I see the book *Yellow House* by Sarah Broom right there [on the Pickus Library shelf], that's the book that won the National Book Award, that book is amazing. Sarah wrote at least four books in one and it feels like one book as opposed to four separate books. *Say Nothing* was another book that made. . . . [That's weird, you all got all the books]. *Say Nothing* is another book that made our short list, which is just absolutely incredible. *Midnight in Chernobyl*, that was one of the books that we loved. I'm teaching this book called *Heads of the Colored People* by Nafissa Thompson-Spires, which is just great. I'm teaching *Friday Black*, which is like a satire. Damon Young has this incredible book, *What Doesn't Kill You Makes You Blacker*. He's doing amazing stuff with the essay form. I've been reading a lot of poetry. I reread a lot of books, so *The Color Purple* now is the book that I'm just still obsessed with how she pulled that off. I don't know if you all read that book, but that book is a monster, man. I don't know how she did that thing.

Jesmyn Ward. I feel lucky enough to come from Mississippi, I feel lucky enough to be writing at the same time that Jesmyn's writing. Morrison, I think she's the greatest fiction writer. To me, she's one of the top five fiction writers of all time, and I've been reading a lot more and more since she passed. Trying to reread and understand some of the stuff I didn't understand before. I don't feel like you can ever reread *Beloved* enough times, but it's a scary book, so I understand why people don't.

SP: Who is your favorite fictional character and why?

KL: That is a great question. I'm going to sound like a complete narcissist, but I don't care this is my honest to God answer. When I wrote this book called *Long Division*, it was the first book I wrote. There's a long story behind that, but anyway, the book came out and it wasn't ever edited. If that book could've been edited it could've been a monster. But there's a character I write about in there, her name is Baize, and to me she actually is the writer of the book, but she's just this massively complicated young Black girl from Mississippi who lost her parents in Katrina. She's a writer, she's a rapper, her tongue is real quick. She's trying to figure out what to do with trauma, how to use trauma to make art. She honestly. . . . She haunts me, I dream about this character. I'm doing this new novel, she comes up in it. She to me is. . . . Oh man, I hate saying some character I wrote, but she's just the most interesting character that I've ever read. I don't know if you've ever experienced this, but if you've ever read pieces of your work and you're like, "Damn, did I write that?" And sometimes like, "Aw shit, did I write that? That's terrible." But for her, every time I read her I just feel like there was something else guiding the writing of it. I knew I had to write it, but it just feels like she wrote herself onto the page. So Baize, Baize Shephard would be my favorite literary character.

SP: What does ethics in today's world mean to you?

KL: It's tough, right? Because you want to be like, "What should it mean? What could it mean?" But your question is What does it mean? I don't know why, but ethics feels like the opportunity to actually put ourselves in relationship to big moral ideas. And to wholeheartedly wrestle with how we actually think about big ideas, as opposed to just the regurgitation of the big idea. I think an ethic, and ethics, necessitate individuals considering who they are, how they are, what they can be in relationship to morality, anti-Blackness, environmental degradation. It's not just what those things mean, it's actually who you are. I was talking to students today, they had a lot of critiques of Duke, and my question was, "Ethically though, do you want Duke to fundamentally change the way you want it to change if that change means that Duke then becomes less of a passport to power for you, or less salient?" I'm interested in how the individual and the idea honestly, not truthfully, but honestly reckon and tangle. And for me, ethics is that. That's a big ole' question.

The Flag and the Fury

Radiolab/WNYC Studios / 2020

From the *Radiolab Podcast*, July 12, 2020. Reprinted with permission of *Radiolab*/WNYC Studios.

Rather than being a traditional interview, Kiese Laymon is conversing with several people on *Radiolab*'s "The Flag and the Fury" episode regarding the resolution to change Mississippi's state flag. In addition to several important quotes by Laymon, the episode features a lot of contextual information and background on the state flag. Laymon's commentary is interspersed throughout with other commentary.

Jad Abumrad: Before we start, this podcast contains a fair amount of strong language.
[Radiolab *Intro*]
Kiese Laymon: I pledge to never be passive, patriotic, or grateful in the face of American abuse. I pledge to always thoughtfully bite the self-righteous American hand that thinks it's feeding us. I pledge that white Mississippians and white Americans will never dictate who I choose to be or what symbols I choose imbue with meaning. I pledge to not allow American ideals of patriotism and masculinity to make me hard, abusive, generic, and brittle. I pledge to messily love our people and myself better than I did yesterday. I pledge to be the kind of free that makes justly winning and gently losing possible. To never ever confuse cowardice with courage. I pledge allegiance to the Mississippi freedom fighters who made all my pledges possible. I pledge allegiance to the baby Mississippi liberation fighters coming next. This is my pledge of allegiance to my United States of America and to my Mississippi. Ready or not, this is a pledge to my home. Are y'all standing up?
[**Archive clip, politician:** *The resolution passes.*]
[**Archive clip, politician:** *History will be made here today.*]
JA: Okay. Mississippi.

[*Archive clip, Roy Wilkins:* A savage, uncivilized state.]
JA: A state of extremes.
[*Archive clip, RW:* Murder and racial hatred.]
[*Archive clip, singing:* In Jackson, Mississippi.]
JA: The state where Emmett Till was brutally murdered. Medgar Evers was assassinated.
[*Archive clip:* And shot in the back by a single round from a high-powered rifle.]
JA: The state with the highest number of lynchings in the Union, but also a staggeringly high number of Nobel, Pulitzer Prize, and National Book Award winners. The most charitable state in the Union. Mississippi is also the state with the highest percentage of Black people in America. And for the last 126 years, Mississippi has had a Confederate battle flag on their state flag. Sort of upper left-hand corner. Red, white and blue stripes, Confederate battle flag upper left. Other states like South Carolina and Georgia would fly the Confederate flag on their state capitols, but one by one they took them off. Mississippi was the last holdout. Until last week. You might have heard about this on the news. I want to tell you the story behind this deflagging. It's an amazing story. Something we've been following for months, because . . .
[*Archive clip, man:* Leave our flag alone!]
JA: It's way more than just another story about taking down a thing.
[*Archive clip, woman:* Just because we've had it for years, doesn't mean we need to keep it.]
JA: This is a journey that involves a clash of histories.
[*Archive clip, man:* Honor!]
[*Archive clip, man:* Outright hate.]
[*Archive clip, man:* Freedom!]
JA: Designs.
[*Archive clip, man:* Just hate.]
[*Archive clip, man:* And courage!]
[*Archive clip, man:* Just hate.]
JA: Generations.
[*Archive clip, man:* There will be retribution.]
JA: And philosophies about how to make change. This is a story that I've been working on with my Dolly Parton's *America* colleague Shima Oliaee. She'll start us off.
Shima Oliaee: Okay, so story starts in a sea of red.

Clara Justus: It was just as far as the eye could see, Confederate flags. In the stands instead of pom-poms, you'd see the flag waving like it was a pom-pom. And then if they didn't have a flag they would take their shirts off and pin them on their bodies. It was like a sea of Confederate flags. But we just kind of saw it as, that's their symbol.

SO: Can you just say your full name and. . . .

CJ: Okay, so Clara Justus. And I'm the vice president of Business Complete Solutions in San Diego.

SO: The place that Clara's talking about is the University of Mississippi or Ole Miss. This is a place where during football games they would roll out a Confederate flag that was as big as the football stand.

CJ: It was massive.

Ashton Pittman: The second biggest Confederate flag in the country.

SO: That's Ashton Pittman.

AP: Senior reporter at the Mississippi Free Press.

JA: What's the biggest?

AP: I do not know what the first is, but it was—if you walked around, cheerleaders carrying Confederate flags, but it was everywhere.

SO: But then the first domino falls.

John Hawkins: Would it be better for me to use my microphone as well?

SO: Maybe. Well, you're using your cellphone, right?

JH: I'm gonna record it with my mic, but I can—you tell me.

SO: The movement to de-Dixie the Mississippi state flag, it is a long, convoluted, confusing, many-headed history. But you could argue that it really goes back to one guy: John Hawkins, Ole Miss class of 1984.

JH: I had a lot of different hats when I was at Ole Miss. Aside from being a student, I was busy when I arrived on campus trying to figure out how to get on the basketball team. Because I had been a pretty good high school player, a great scorer, and of course, you know, as fate would have it I got injured, wasn't as good a basketball player as I thought I was and went off to do some other things.

SO: John got involved with student government.

JH: Yeah, I became president of the Black student body.

SO: He was on all kinds of committees, was in a Black fraternity. He was basically a man about campus. Now just for context. . . .

JH: We only had about five-hundred Black students in the whole campus of what, 13,000? So what's that percentage-wise? Two percent, maybe three percent?

SO: Closer to eight, but still....

JH: So it was a really small number, so there never....

SO: And you've got to keep in mind that this was only twenty years after a man by the name of James Meredith....

[*News clip:* James H. Meredith.]

SO: ... became the first Black student to enter the University of Mississippi.

AP: And....

[*News clip:* The town becomes an armed battlefield.]

AP: President Kennedy had to send the National Guard.

[*News clip:* Armed with tear gas and sidearms.]

AP: ... over that.

[*News clip:* Two men are killed, hundred and fifty are arrested after a night of terror.]

SO: Thousands of federal troops, days of riots. It was rough. In any case, one day in John's sophomore year he's sitting in a Black Student Committee meeting and they're discussing the cheerleading squad. There had never been a Black cheerleader at Ole Miss in its 134 years of existence.

JH: And my good friend Clara Bibbs....

Clara Bibbs: There we go.

JH: ... who had always wanted to be an Ole Miss cheerleader, she....

CB: So I was like, gonna be trying out.

JH: ... her partner, who was helping her try out was a white male, which was in and of itself kind of unheard of at that time at Ole Miss, but it just spoke to the fact that things were starting to change on campus.

CB: Yes.

SO: Problem was the white guy gets injured, and now Clara had no partner.

JH: She was in the lurch about two weeks or so before tryouts. And we were having this committee meeting trying to determine okay, so what can we do? You know, Clara's our best hope to ever achieve this. We just didn't have a solution. And someone [*laughs*] asked me if I would consider doing it, because I mean I was athletic enough...

CB: He was—he's very tall and he's very strong. I'm, like, 5′1″ and a half. John has to be 6′2″, maybe 6′3″.

JH: I mean, I never knew anything about cheerleading. I knew that, you know, Clara weighed about 110–15 pounds and, you know, in the weight room back in those days I could throw 115 pounds around all day. So....

JA: Okay.

JH: ... so I ended up saying, "Yeah, sure. I'll help her."

CB: Right.

SO: So for two weeks, John and Clara met up, practiced. . . .

[*Archive clip, JH:* One of the fun aspects of learning to be a cheerleader for the first time is learning how to do partner steps.]

SO: He crammed to learn all the moves.

CB: Like what they call a chair extension.

SO: Where she stands in front of him, he puts his hands. . . .

CB: . . . on your waist.

[*Archive clip, JH:* She gives a little jump.]

SO: She hops up.

CB: The guy takes his right hand and puts it under your butt.

SO: And she's sort of lifted up into the air to sit on his hand that's held high above his head.

CB: He holds your other left leg with his hand.

[*Archive clip, JH:* High on the thigh, above the knee. Never on the knee.]

CB: It was a lot of lifting of me. A lot of picking up.

JH: You know, pick up the girl, throw the girl as high as you can, catch the girl, and don't let her get hurt. Keep in mind, back in these days Ole Miss was the national cheerleading champion.

CB: Very competitive.

JH: So being an Ole Miss cheerleader was a big deal.

SO: Anyhow, John got up to speed and the two of them try out for judges along with hundreds of other mostly white students. And then. . . .

JH: There was this kind of fate that threw us a curveball because, you know, the process at Ole Miss was a little bit stacked.

CB: Right, right, right. So the way the cheerleading squad at Ole Miss worked is that. . . .

JH: There was a qualifying process.

CB: . . . you had to try out.

JH: You'd have this huge tryout, where it would get narrowed down to. . . .

CB: . . . the top ten.

JH: . . . the top ten males and the top ten females. Well as fate would have it, we both make the top ten. We both make the cut.

SO: Oh, wow!

JA: Wow, that must've been a pretty big deal!

JH: Yeah. And that in and of itself was phenomenal.

SO: The complication was how the process worked is that after that first cut . . .

CB: Then it went to a vote.

SO: A popular vote.

JH: So once you've gone through the gauntlet and demonstrated that you had the ability, it then became a popularity contest on campus where you then had to go out and campaign and get your groups of friends, fraternities, sororities, whatever to vote you in.

CB: So the votes were paper. Just by word of mouth.

JH: Of course you know who I was campaigning for. [*Laughs*]

JA: Right.

JH: I was campaigning for Clara and trying to see if we could get her on that squad.

SO: But John was a very visible guy.

CB: Whereas I was the opposite. You know, I was a journalist, wasn't in any sororities.

SO: To make a long story short . . .

JH: I ended up getting elected.

CB: But I didn't.

JA: Oh, that's complicated!

JH: Yeah, it was—it was a real complicated issue.

JA: What were the conversations with Clara like right after that?

JH: It was devastating, because I didn't want to do it. I mean, I was only there for her.

CB: I was at a friend's house and someone called me. I was like, "Okay. I didn't make it. Not a big deal." I think everybody was just in shock. Like, wait a minute. This wasn't how it was supposed to go. [*Laughs*] They were like, "It wasn't supposed to go down like this. How did this happen?" I think is kind of how everybody looked at it, and they were—they kind of looked at me like, "Oh my God, we're so sorry!" I'm like, "Don't be sorry." You have to understand coming out of Jim Crow, I wasn't used to things going my way anyway.

SO: Clara told us she grew up in a rural town in Central Mississippi, that even as late as 1976—1976!—had separate entrances for Black and white citizens.

SO: And you guys—and just to be clear, you guys never talked it out at that time?

CB: No, we didn't.

JH: Because I mean, even before she and I could have that conversation about what does it mean and so forth, the evening of the election. . . .

SO: April 22, 1982.

JH: It was such a momentous occasion. . . .

SO: John says initially the vibe was positive.

JH: There was a great spirit on campus. Both, you know, Black and white kids really were celebrating that achievement in and of itself.

SO: Reporters, though, chased him around campus, finally cornered him in the student union, and then began to bombard him with some difficult questions.

CB: After that I'm thinking, "Holy cow! You know, what did—what did I get him into?"

SO: One reporter asked would he be comfortable with a white, female partner as the ghost of Emmett Till entered the room. Apparently, John answers, "This is a new age, and the time has passed for prejudice."

JH: And of course that's when the infamous question comes up, when someone asks me about the Confederate flag and if I was gonna follow Ole Miss tradition and wave the rebel flag.

SO: That's how every game started, with male cheerleaders running out and waving a giant battle flag.

JH: Listen to me, I never expected to have to answer that question.

SO: John said he literally had never contemplated it, because he never thought he'd be a cheerleader to begin with. And that moment, between when he was asked the question and when he answered, a few things went through his mind. He thought about his grandmother.

JH: She died when she was 102 years old.

SO: Wow!

JH: So imagine this for a moment: This is my grandmother. Not my great-great-grandmother. This is my grandmother, whose mother was born a slave.

SO: He thought about the fact that when he got chosen for the cheerleading squad, he suddenly started seeing a whole lot more of those rebel flags being carried around campus, almost as if they came out in reaction to his presence. He thought about how the tuition he paid helped . . .

JH: . . . buy those flags that we had no interest in. And so when the question came up about the flag . . .

SO: He says he just looked at the reporters square in the eyes and said. . . .

JH: I said, "Of course not." The answer was no.

JA: And that just came out? That wasn't premeditated?

JH: No, it was instinctive. I had—hadn't even thought about it.

CB: For a Black person like John to carry the Confederate flag is like a Jewish person carrying a swastika.

SO: From the moment he said no, the story exploded.

JH: Went the equivalent of viral. Keep in mind, this is before social media.

[***News clip:*** *The Confederate flag is at the heart of an emotional racial dispute at the University of Mississippi.*]

JH: We talk about agitation [*laughs*] in the context of George Floyd, no, I know—I can tell you what agitation looks like.

[***News clip:*** *The flag of the Confederacy has always been the cause of not-so-subtle agitation, but those feelings had been unspoken until the university's first Black cheerleader refused to carry the flag.*]

JH: People were leading hostile protests on the campus.

SO: John received death threats.

[***News clip:*** *The Ku Klux Klan held an off-campus march in protest.*]

SO: Someone set his dorm room on fire.

Curtis "Pedee" Scott: Probably was the most hated person in the South, you know? [*Laughs*]

SO: This is Curtis "PEDEE" Scott. He was in John's fraternity at the time.

CPS: John and I was best friends, and they was two doors down.

SO: He told me the story about just how bad things got. There was one night he says when they were all at the fraternity house . . .

CPS: And the police came in and said, "We want you all to turn off the light, get down on the floor." And we was like, "What is going on?" All of a sudden, we could hear the chants coming from afar, and it was getting louder and louder. So, you know, we looked out there and we saw the mob marching down Jackson Street.

[***News clip:*** *1,000 white students held a noisy rally in support of the flag earlier this week.*]

[***News clip:*** *Flag-waving white students marched on a Black fraternity house.*]

CPS: I will never forget the chant. "We want Hawkins! We want Hawkins!" It was almost as though they wanted to break in the house or either want us to get John and throw him to the mob.

SO: Curtis says Black students from around the campus started running to the fraternity house to defend them, but the police stopped them.

CPS: Thank God that didn't happen because that would have been a horrible scene. I mean, it would've been totally horrible.

JH: You know, state police was called out at one point.

CPS: State troopers, city police.

SO: Which reminded a lot of people of 1962.

JH: Mobs came out, stopped traffic.

[***News clip:*** *Black students held a counter-demonstration, demanding that the university find another symbol.*]

JH: That really carried through into the full year. When I was on the squad, game days were [*laughs*] were quite interesting.

SO: John says before games they'd take him from a safe house, sneak him into the stadium where he'd then lead cheers for people who booed him.

JA: Wow. It must've been really lonely standing on that field.

JH: [*Laughs*] Well, not only on that field, but on every field every time we showed up for a football game.

SO: After twelve football games of this, twenty-something basketball games, continued protests, counter-protests, the chancellor of the school. . . .

CPS: I think his name was Porter.

SO: . . . a man named Porter Fortune, issued a statement.

[***Archive clip, Porter Fortune:*** *If there is a feeling that racism exists on our campus, I want to be the first to attempt to get rid of it.*]

CPS: The mob, they marched on his mansion. [*Laughs*] So, you know, so he probably was like, "What do I need to do? I feel like my life is in jeopardy now."

[***News clip:*** *And as a result, the flag has been dropped as the school's symbol.*]

JA: Can you read that article from April 23, 1983?

JH: You know I'm an old man now, so if I can get my glasses if I need them. "But the Chancellor of the University of Mississippi trying to defuse a race—a racial dispute said yesterday the Confederate flag would no longer be used as a school symbol." This was the lightning rod event.

SO: The NAACP for years had been thinking about starting a campaign against the display of the Confederate flag. They wanted to take this down. But they thought there was no way it could ever happen in Mississippi. It took this one guy to say, "No, I'm not gonna wave the flag" for everyone to just ponder the idea that it could be possible.

JH: When I've subsequently talked to Clara, you know, I think she's even said that, "You know, maybe God chose you for that moment moreso than me because He knew that you can handle it."

CB: I think in hindsight, that was—that was meant to be. It was meant to be that way. He stood his ground, he didn't carry it. He didn't let them push him off the squad. I don't know that I would have had that strength. So I'm glad it was John.

JH: You know, sometimes the universe lines up in such a way that it's the time for change.

JA: It's so weird to be talking to you right at this minute, because right now literally as we are doing this interview, the Mississippi state legislature is meeting and they may be about to take down the flag.

Laurin Stennis: I just got a text from a senator saying in ten minutes, like—literally, like, in five minutes the flag could go down.

JH: Well, hopefully they'll do the right thing.

JA: Yeah.

JH: It's long overdue.

JA: So in 1983, the University of Ole Miss decides no more Confederate flags can be flown at Ole Miss. This was the first domino. But it was only a baby domino.

[***News clip:*** *The white students applauded the chancellor's decision to permit individuals to carry the flag.*]

JH: He's trying to thread the needle, right?

[***Archive clip, woman:*** *As long as I can bring it to the game, I don't care.*]

JA: And the even trickier part was, since the Confederate flag was actually embedded in the Mississippi state flag and had been since 1894, and since Ole Miss was a state institution, the Confederate battle flag was still there by default in front of the school administration buildings flapping in the breeze, and would remain that way for another thirty-two years. Until. . . .

[***News clip:*** *It is a heartbreaking videotape taken just before the church massacre that shocked the world.*

JA: 2015, a deranged racist walks into a historic Black church in South Carolina, kills nine people, and is later found in an old photograph to be holding the Confederate battle flag.

[***News clip:*** *Last night, the University of Mississippi Student Government Association voted to remove the flag bearing the Confederate battle emblem.*]

JA: The school then finally decides they cannot fly the state flag.

[***News clip:*** *The recent racially motivated church shootings in South Carolina giving momentum to those who want it taken down.*]

JA: So at this point, the flagpoles are empty. And not just at Ole Miss. All across the state you begin to see businesses removing the Mississippi state flag. Question was: What to put in its place? And that's when you start to see another flag being hoisted. And this brings us to Chapter Two.

LS: Ooh.

JA: To Laurin.

LS: Here we go. Give me a hug—oh, we can't do that. [*Laughs*]

JA: We Zoomed with Laurin Stennis for the first time back in April.

LS: Oh hell, stop! Roomba just came on. [*Laughs*]

JA: Oh really? Oh, I just met my first Roomba just a couple days ago. They're so loud.

LS: Damn you, Roomba!

JA: It was early pandemic, Laurin was quarantined in her home/art studio in Jackson, Mississippi with her cat and dog and Roomba. Her journey to the center of the Mississippi flag fight takes a very different trajectory than John's.

LS: Yes, ma'am.

JA: Around the same time that he was stepping foot on Ole Miss campus for the first time, she was talking to birds.

LS: Well, my mother fed birds when I was growing up and, you know, these goldfinches that are just stunning when they're in their summer plumage. I just was entranced as a kid, and—to the point that I started thinking birds were talking to me. [*Laughs*] But there's a pill for that, yeah. [*Laughs*]

JA: Laurin says her childhood was pretty idyllic.

LS: I would lay down in the middle of clover and watch clouds. I would get little locust shells off the trees. You know, played in the creeks and looked at tadpoles.

JA: And when you were that young, like seven or eight, did you have any concept of—that your grandfather was who he was?

LS: Not exactly. I really had no sense of kind of who my grandfather was in the larger sense.

JA: Laurin's grandfather, by the way....

[**News clip:** *Speaking with United States Senator John C. Stennis of Mississippi.*]

JA: ... is John Stennis. Or was John Stennis, he died in 1995. Southern Democrat who served in the Senate for over forty-one years. And for much of that time....

[**Archive clip, John C. Stennis:** *We gone to the extreme on civil rights. We've just let it run away.*]

JA: ... he was a staunch segregationist.

[**Archive clip, JCS:** *No doubt.*]

LS: I think I became conscious of that probably in high school, really.

JA: I'm curious what that was like to learn that, because if you read his early letters....

[**Archive clip, JCS:** *Colored people on the employment list.*]

JA: ... he talks really openly about how he believes Black people are inferior....

[**Archive clip, JCS:** *And we've let them do largely as they wanted to do and didn't punish them.*]

JA: ... the fact that he opposed the Voting Rights Act, the Civil Rights Act....

[*Archive clip, JCS:* They must be stopped if we have personal liberty and freedom left for anyone.]

JA: ... even a holiday for Martin Luther King.

[*Archive clip, JCS:* And I'm certain in my belief.]

JA: How do you process that, given that, given what you believe and also the fact that he is your grandfather?

LS: I mean, you know, hearing and reading various things, you know, I get a little nauseated to be honest. It's twofold. One, because that's just such a revolting belief. But that I'm related—you know, that he was a white guy born in 1901, less than forty years after the Civil War in a rural, unincorporated town. You know, I mean it's like, am I shocked? No.

JA: Hmm.

LS: I mean, I'm able to see him in his context. I would love it if he had been this amazing, you know, guy who was able to transcend everything he was taught and, you know, came out as this early progressive leader. It was wrong. It's indefensible. But am I shocked? Not particularly.

JA: Laurin's political awakening and subsequent interest in flags was slow to take by her own admission. After high school, she went to Tulane.

LS: I left Tulane with a 1.7 GPA because I just quit going to class. I think at that point I was just kind of raging against the machine, and I didn't even fully understand what the machine was and that really I was part of it.

JA: She says she started to see and understand that machine when she transferred from Tulane to Millsaps back in Mississippi, and then fell into a rabbit hole of ethics classes and women's studies courses, and soon began to write cutting essays about politics for an alt-progressive newspaper.

Kiese Laymon: We were just—we were initially just shocked that someone who came from what appeared to us to be, like, such voracious racist beginnings could give her, at that point, twenty-one—twenty-two-year-old life to causes that would probably make her grandfather, like, squeal.

JA: This is author Kiese Laymon again, who started us off with that alternative pledge. He and Laurin worked on that paper together at Millsaps and they politically organized together.

KL: You know, growing up we were always kind of taught that there was a group of people called good white folks, and those were....

LS: [*Laughs*]

KL: ... you know, and you questioned the motives of good white folks. But you know, once somebody, like, bleeds over into that category, like, you know, we knew early on that Laurin was good white folk.

JA: Okay, so let's jump forward to your flag. When did you begin that journey?

LS: It started when I moved back.

JA: This is after she had gone to school, moved away, become a social worker and an artist and then returned.

LS: Bought a little house and just instinctively, you know, it was like I'm home and I was excited and I was proud and I liked my little house and I wanted to put out a flag.

JA: Huh.

LS: You know, I'm back in Mississippi. And I would never, never have our current state flag. And I just—I just kind of sat down and just thought, "This is ridiculous. This is absurd that Mississippians didn't have a flag that anyone can fly without a moment's hesitation." So after reflecting on that, I began to do some research. So I ended up down at archives.

JA: She said she just wanted to know if there were other options out there besides the 1894 Mississippi state flag with the Confederate battle flag on it. And she says the first thing that she encountered was that there was a flag before that flag.

LS: The Magnolia flag, as it was called. This was the flag that people said was the first state flag of Mississippi.

JA: It was created in 1861. What you see is a white background and cartoonish green tree in the middle.

LS: It's like, it's so ugly it's cute. Because I mean, the magnolia tree is a blob.

KL: Yeah, it just looks like a—it looked like an afro. It looked like a big-ass green afro. Like a wopped—what we used to call, like, a wopped afro.

SO: What's a wopped afro?

KL: Like an afro. You know, afro's supposed to be round, you know? When we used to have 'fros, like our 'fro sometimes wouldn't be, like, round. They'd be, like, off to the side if you fell asleep or. . . .

JA: [*Laughs*]

SO: [*Laughs*]

KL: It just—it just wasn't—I mean, to me that's the first thing I thought. I was like, "Oh, that shit looks like an afro in the middle but it's not shaped right."

JA: Okay, so Laurin initially thought, "Oh, I'll just fly the Magnolia flag." Problem is. . . .

LS: It was commissioned and designed for the newly seceded Republic of Mississippi of 1861.

JA: Oh.

SO: Oh, wow.

JA: There you go. Okay.

LS: And I was like, "Uh-uh."

JA: At a certain point Laurin just thought, "Well, I'm an artist. Let me see what I can come up with."

LS: I—I started to kind of doodle. I started to—because I knew flags that I love. Like, Tennessee has a great flag. Colorado, New Mexico. You know, I knew good flags when I saw them and I thought, "What is it?"

JA: That question led her to the wonderful world of vexillology.

LS: It took me forever to be able to say it, but it's the study of flags.

JA: There's a whole field of study about flags?

LS: It is primarily a bunch of old white guys. . . .

[**Archive clip, man:** *This is a flag.*]

LS: . . . that'll mansplain. . . .

[**Archive clip, man:** *And this is a flag.*]

LS: . . . to you to death.

[**Archive clip, man:** *And this is a flag. And this is a flag.*]

LS: They were so excited when I joined the North American Vexillological Association. I was certainly, I think, the youngest member. And yeah, one of their only female members.

[**Archive clip, man:** *And this is a flag.*]

JA: She ultimately got to work coming up with a design that looks a little like a deconstructed remixed American flag. You've got three vertical stripes, red, white, red.

LS: And the red color really symbolizes the blood spilled by Mississippians who have given their lives for liberty and justice.

JA: In the middle of the flag you have a circle of stars.

LS: When I was looking at Indigenous art among tribes that were native to Mississippi even before statehood, I would see a circular or a spiral element in some of the work.

JA: The circle, she says, was a nod to them, also to the endless cycles of history.

LS: You know, no beginning, no end.

JA: There are precisely nineteen stars in the circle for the nineteen states that joined the Union before Mississippi. And inside the circle . . .

LS: The star in the middle is the twentieth, and it's the biggest and the best, and that's us.

JA: Laurin took that mock-up and sent it to a guy . . .

Ted Kaye: Recording starting now.

JA: . . . named Ted Kaye.

TK: I'm the Secretary of the North American Vexillological Association.

SO: He's famous in the flag world.

LA: Yeah. He's a god.

SO: Ted literally wrote the book *Good Flag, Bad Flag*, where he outlines the five principals of good flag design.

TK: Simplicity, meaningful symbolism, few colors, no lettering or seals and distinctiveness.

LA: So I emailed him and said, "You don't know me from Adam's housecat, but here's what I have and I would love your feedback." And he was so kind and so generous. He wrote back and he said, "I love your design. All I would do is make the stars . . ."

TK: Bigger.

LA: ". . . bigger."

TK: As big as you can get them.

LS: "You know, but you've got a top-ten flag design, top-ten United States flag design here. It's great."

TK: It may well be showing Mississippians that a different flag could represent the state.

LS: "And good luck with that."

TK: But I've had informal conversations with at least five different people who are working on proposed flags in Mississippi.

JA: Like—like, recently?

TK: In the last couple years, yes.

JA: Having a good design, says Ted, is just the beginning. And there's a lot more to flags than what's on them. In our conversation, he walked us through the long history of flags and I gotta say it sort of put the whole Mississippi flag fight in a new context.

TK: Flags started out as markers on the battlefield. And this was true all the way up through the Civil War. It's very important to know where your troops are on the battlefield, and they are marked by flags.

SO: Imagine, he says, two armies face off. It's a melee. The sides get confused and you need to regroup. You look for the flag and you run to the flag.

TK: So it's important to have someone carry that flag. And one of the problems when you're carrying a flag is you can't shoot back. You are defenseless and everybody wants to shoot at you because if you can knock down the enemy's flag, you reduce their ability to know where their troops are. So the culture of the military was to imbue great honor in being the flag-bearer because that's what you needed to do to get someone to sacrifice. There are stories of battles in the Civil War where there would be one charge across the battlefield. One would be shot, the next guy would pick it up. He'd be shot, the next guy would pick it up. He'd be shot. Six people would die carrying that flag. So it's very important in military propaganda I would say to have people feel strongly about the flag.

JA: Oh, that's so interesting! Like, in some sense the way in which we revere and honor and sing to and then fight over the flag is a direct spiritual line back to the battlefield.

TK: It could well be.

SO: Add to that, he says, in America we don't have a king or queen. We put all of that deference up on our flag. And you feel the emotional weight of that when you look back to 2001.

[**Archive clip, Ronnie Musgrove:** *Governor Tuck, Mr. Speaker, members of the Mississippi Legislature, Chief Justice Pittman . . .*]

SO: After years of people submitting bills to change the flag that went absolutely nowhere, in 1988, 1990, 1992, 1993, the governor at the time, Ronnie Musgrove. . . .

[**Archive clip, RM:** *I implore you to hear our people again.*]

SO: . . . urged the legislature to give the decision to the people. . . .

[**Archive clip, RM:** *I urge you to put this issue on the ballot.*]

SO: . . . in a referendum. And leading up to that vote there were a series of town halls across Mississippi.

[**News clip:** *Tonight's first Friday flag special features a representative sampling of the views expressed by Mississippians at the five public hearings dealing with the future of Mississippi's flag.*]

SO: You can watch these town halls online. They took place in auditoriums, church basements. And they are—well, they're battles.

[**Archive clip, man:** *Where does it stop?*]

[**Archive clip, man:** *So we are tired of this onslaught against the Confederate heritage. It needs to stop and it needs to stop right now.*]

[**Archive clip, man:** *Our state flag represents grit, guts, and cajones! Our state flag—our state flag represents pride!*]

[**Archive clip, man:** *You white people don't get it!*]

[**Archive clip, man:** *This is the year 2000! We will not go back. We will not go back. That flag must be changed. I've lived all over the country. We are the laughingstock of America. That flag represents Mississippi being fifty* in education. Fifty in per-capita income. Number one in infant mortality. Number one in lynching. We cannot afford to keep that flag. We must move forward!]

[**Archive clip, man:** *This flag is just like my wife. You mess with my wife, you'll get your ass kicked! That's all there is to it.*]

[**Archive clip, man:** *Our state flag—you listen up. You listenin' over there? Our state flag represents blood, sweat and tears of countless Southerners who are a far sight better than any of y'all. Now listen, Mr. Winter?*]

SO: Mr. Winter was the head of the flag commission, former governor. He was in the room.

[**Archive clip, man:** *You are despicable. You are an anathema. You are an anathema to what is honorable in this state!*]

[Cheering]

[**Archive clip, man:** *You have—hey, hey! No, no, no, no, no. It's my time! My time!*]

[Jeering]

[**Archive clip, man:** *Hey listen, listen. You have been nothing but a parasite your entire career. You're a sorry lawyer. You're gutless. You are worthy of being tarred and feathered and run out of this state.*]

[Cheering]

SO: It goes on and on like this. One of the craziest moments in a sea of crazy is when a seventeen-year-old white girl with bright orange hair steps up to the mic.

[**Archive clip, girl:** *I am a young girl working in a grocery store environment. I do work with Blacks and I have several—not just one or two, but several friends who are Black. One person said, "Where would the slaves in America be today if it weren't for slavery?" They'd probably still be in Africa enslaved. Or other European nations. Another person asked me to point out most—not all—of the African American race living in America today got their last name from their masters. Are you prepared to give up your name? I don't think you are. Because if you get my flag I will get your name. (SCREAMING) Wait, I'm not finished! Take your pick and get out!*]

SO: So that was 2001. And before we get back to Laurin, as you watch these videos one thing that you can't help but ask yourself is, "Where do some of these people get these ideas from?"

Ashton Pittman: Right. But I will say that....

SO: This is a question that Ashton Pittman, the reporter we spoke to earlier, asked himself. And he started to actually track down some of the people in the video, including the orange-haired girl, who by the way is a radiologist today and was valedictorian of her high school class. And what he discovered is that most of them went to what's called segregation academies.

AP: Yes. Almost all of them were set up in either 1969, 1970, or 1971. I mean, this Supreme Court ruling . . .

[***News clip:*** *The school desegregation ordered in Mississippi began today.*]

AP: . . . to desegregate the public schools came in December 1969.

[***News clip:*** *Reaction to the ruling was predictable, angry and swift.*]

AP: By the start of the school year . . .

[***News clip:*** *The whites are abandoning the public schools.*]

AP: January of 1970. . . .

[***News clip:*** *Private schools are appearing in great numbers.*]

AP: . . . you had white kids not returning to their public schools and going to makeshift schools that were set up in white churches. . . .

[***News clip:*** *White volunteers are converting a tent factory into classrooms.*]

AP: . . . or in makeshift buildings.

[***News clip:*** *Many of these schools represent a last resort for white parents determined to resist federal desegregation orders.*]

AP: Like, that's the origin of a ton of these academies. I think at one point there were like. . . .

[***News clip:*** *And one estimate is they number in the thousands.*]

JA: Wow.

AP: Yeah. They went up overnight. So if you make sure your kids only go to white schools with other white kids, you don't have to worry about, you know, maybe your kids developing some empathy for their Black classmates, having a greater understanding of viewpoints that are outside of that kind of white supremacist mindset. And in 2001—and still today, honestly—a lot of these private academies that popped up in 1970, 1971, even in 2001, a lot of them were still either all white or, you know, 99, 98 percent white. And that's still true today.

SO: In fact, Ashton told us that he and his husband William found that over a third of the current Mississippi senators today attended segregation academies.

JA: In any case, in that 2001 referendum. . . .

[***News clip:*** *Sixty-four percent chose the 1894 flag over the alternative.*]

JA: Mississippi voted to keep the state flag, Confederate battle flag and all.

LS: And people were like, well, 65 percent of the people in Mississippi voted to keep the flag. No, 65 percent of the people who showed up that day, but only 23 percent of our population showed up to vote that day.

JA: Suffice to say, the vote went along racial lines. But the mostly white proflag contingent, unsurprisingly, had better turnout.

LS: At that point, I will admit, I got—it was a little daunting.

JA: As Laurin was doodling new flag designs, rooting around in the archives and reading all the letters people sent during that 2001 referendum, she started to wonder, how do you prevent that from happening again? I mean, obviously part of it is entrenched and systemic. Part of it, it occurred to her, was just a pattern that she had seen in her social work, where one person saying "Stop," only causes the person they're saying it to to dig in harder.

LS: This is kind of where the psychology part comes in. I began to realize that many of the other previous efforts took the angle of trying to shame some Mississippians.

JA: Mm-hmm.

LS: Psychologically, if you're saying—yeah, that's the hashtag that a lot of people were using.

[*Archive clip, protesters: Take it down! Take it down! Take it down!*]

LS: "Take it down, take it down, take it down." Now, psychologically, if you're saying I'm going to take something from you, even if you're not that attached to it. . . .

SO: [*Laughs*] That's so true.

LS: . . . you might start to squeeze it a little bit.

[*Archive clip, man: This flag is just like my wife!*]

LS: And be like, "No, wait a minute."

[*Archive clip, man: You mess with my wife, you'll get your ass kicked!*]

LS: The psychology of loss is really strong. But if I'm offering you something and I'm doing something positive and I'm not threatening you, it just makes sense. And so my—my—my hashtag has been #PutItUp.

JA: Okay, so 2015 after Laurin had designed her flag, workshopped it a bit with Ted Kaye, she puts the design on Facebook.

LS: I didn't have any plan at that point.

JA: She said it was just for her friends to see. But then a few things happen. There's the mass shooting at the Black church in South Carolina. Ole Miss then votes to take down the state flag on their campus. And in the wake of that, Laurin gets a message from a state senator saying. . . .

LS: By the way, I just introduced a bill to change the state flag to your flag. And I typed "What?"

SO: Oh, wow!

LS: She had not reached out to me. She had just seen what I was doing on Facebook and was like, "I'm gonna go for it." So that really got the ball rolling.

JA: That particular bill didn't go anywhere.

LS: Once again, all flag bills died in committee.

JA: But. . . .

LS: Oh, game on. So I. . . .

JA: . . . she went ahead and manufactured a bunch of her flags anyway, took 'em to a local flag store in Jackson, Mississippi.

LS: Y'all keep the money. I just—I just ask if you will please make it affordable.

JA: Because this was a moment when business after business was following Ole Miss' lead and taking that state flag down, which left a lot of empty flag poles for her flag to go up. And within a year her flag, which she called the "Mississippi hospitality flag" but everybody else called "the Stennis flag" . . .

LS: It was the number one-selling flag in the state. Which is. . . .

SO: Oh, wow!

JA: She was beginning to outsell the 1894 state flag many times over.

LS: I mean, that—that flag store is making bank! And more and more it's caught on and you see it flying more places. But last—not this current session that got called because of the pandemic but the session before that, I was approached by a Republican lawmaker who said, "Have you thought about doing a specialty license plate?"

JA: Her and this Republican lawmaker cook up a plan that when people order these vanity plates—these are license plates where you have special messages on them—those plates would arrive with her flag on the license plate, rather than the actual state flag.

LS: He said, "Let's just not draw any attention to it." Because it turns out that the way they pass the specialty tags, they group them all together in one bill and just kind of pass them at the end of the session. And so people may or may not read it very carefully. [*Laughs*] So I had to sit on it. I didn't say a word and it passed. We've already raised close to $40,000 for the Mississippi Civil Rights Museum and the Museum of Mississippi History, because I chose them as the recipient for the proceeds.

SO: It's like you guys are leading a quiet revolution.

LS: Well, I would never use the term, like, revolution or whatever because that's threatening to people.

SO: Yeah.

LS: I am—I am way behind the scenes and I'm really quiet, versus when people go, "Change the Flag Rally," I'm like, "Oh shit! Oh shit!"

JA: The whole time that's been Laurin's approach. Keep it stealth. No referendums, no public debates. Just get it out there on cars and banks and fraternities and bars so that people start seeing it.

LS: "Oh yeah, my neighbor has that. Oh yeah, I saw that at Steve's Diner downtown." You know, it's like, that's how it happens. It becomes inevitable. It's like, we're almost there. We're almost there.

KL: I mean, you know, my thing with Laurin is like, I just think she knows white people in a—in a way that I don't. I mean, I think white people have talked to her and said things to her that they've never said to me.

SO: In one my phone calls with Kiese Laymon—Laurin's friend, writer—I asked him what he thinks about the stealth approach.

KL: I'm not gonna say that that's wrong. I just think the interesting thing about Laurin—and this is to her credit, I guess—is that all of her moves seem to be predicated on, like, the POV of the white folks, right?

SO: Hmm.

KL: Like, this is what they'll do, this is what they'll feel, this is what—and I feel that but—but there's a—but there's a large population of the state that is not those people. Do you know what I'm saying? So I'm not trying to disagree with Laurin. She's talking pragmatically, you know what I'm saying? I get it. I feel it. I just can't always be thinking about what—what the racist white people are gonna do.

[*Archive clip, man: The civil rights movement is over!*]

SO: We started talking about those 2001 town hall videos.

[*Archive clip, man: It ended when you started trying to put me down.*]

SO: How if you watch the whole thing, there's a pattern that emerges. You see a lot of Black people dressed in their Sunday best.

[*Archive clip, man: Excuse me. Let me finish talking please, sir. Thank you.*]

SO: And making a deliberate point to speak respectfully and calmly.

[*Archive clip, man: I hope God put on my heart to say something that might change somebody's mind.*]

SO: Whereas, you see a lot of the white people . . .

[*Archive clip, man: [shouting] Our state flag, you listen—you listening over there?*]

SO: Just yelling.

[*Archive clip, woman: All of those reasons. . . .*]

[*Crowd jeering*]

KL: That is why I'm—I literally had to leave because, like, it's humiliating when you always approach these people with that sort of kindness in the face of them telling you that you better fucking shut the fuck up and watch us commemorate your suffering. And where like, I heard what one gentlemen said a few minutes ago. . . .

SO: [*Laughs*] Yes.

KL: . . . about me not being worth a damn. I would just like to—you know what I mean? Like, that's not—that's not—that don't feel natural to me.

SO: One of the things that Kiese is famous for in Mississippi, in addition to his writing, is for getting into a major dust-up at Millsaps with a bunch of white fraternity boys who'd dressed in blackface and Afro wigs and called his girlfriend the n-word.

KL: I'm sure you saw Fannie Lou Hamer when she talked about what happened to her in 1963 in the jail, right? Did you ever see that?

SO: The Fannie Lou Hamer. Is that what you said?

KL: Yeah. Fannie Lou Hamer's speech where she's talking about. . . .

[***Archive clip, Fannie Lou Hamer:*** *I was carried to the county jail and put in the booking room.*]

KL: . . . getting arrested in 1963 and how she was in a jail. And she—she heard another woman down the hall getting beaten.

[***Archive clip, FLH:*** *They beat her, I don't know how long. It wasn't too long before three white men came to my cell.*]

KL: The guards came in and they made Black men beat her damn near to death.

[***Archive clip, FLH:*** *And I laid on my face. The first Negro began to beat me.*]

KL: Fucked up her eye. Fucked up her kidneys.

[***Archive clip, FLH:*** *And I was beat by the first Negro until he was exhausted.*]

KL: I mean, I can't listen to it without crying. Like, she is talking about white men putting her in prison, making Black incarcerated men beat the fuck out of her 'til she's damn near dead.

[***Archive clip, FLH:*** *All of this is on account of we want to register.*]

KL: Just because she wanted the fucking right to vote. But—but the wonder to me, is that she could comport herself to tell that story.

[***Archive clip, FLH:*** *Is this America?*]

KL: You know what I mean? Like, she was so. . . .

[***Archive clip, FLH:*** *The land of the free and the home of the brave?*]

KL: . . . prepared. Even though she's, like, reaching into, like, this well of fucking, like, horror that she should have never had to experience. It is ancestral. Like, people in the face of terror and ultimate fucking humiliation have to comport themselves in particular ways that white folks just never,

ever have to do. And that shit is just foul. Do you know what I mean? Like, that's why at the end of the day, I'm just like, fuck! Yeah. So anyway....

JA: Okay, so up until about a month and a half ago, here's where we were at. You had Laurin quietly campaigning, Kiese wondering if quiet was the way to go. And you had Tate Reeves....

[***News clip:*** *Lieutenant Governor is seen....*]

JA: ... the governor of Mississippi, a guy they both went to school with, and who was actually in that fraternity where the kids wore blackface....

[***News clip:*** *The photos show members of the fraternity in blackface, some holding up a Confederate flag...*]

JA: ... you had him—this is at the beginning of the pandemic—declaring April Confederate History Month. Meanwhile in the legislature, conservative Republicans held—still hold—a supermajority. All of which is to say, that the prospects a month and a half ago of anything happening quickly—or at all—with the state flag were very, very low. But then everything changes. That's after the break.

JA: This is *Radiolab*. I'm Jad Abumrad, here with Shima Oliaee.

SO: Hey!

JA: And we're in the middle of a deep dive into the story behind the removal of the Confederate battle flag-clad Mississippi state flag. Now as we talked about, just a month and a half ago you had a situation where despite Laurin Stennis's best efforts to sneak a new flag into the conversation, despite people like John Hawkins taking a stand against the flag, you had a situation where there was a Republican supermajority in the Senate, a governor who had just declared Confederate Heritage Month. It seemed like if things were gonna change, it was gonna happen really slowly and we'd probably be talking about this for another 126 years.

SO: That is until May 25, 2020.

[***Archive clip, crowd:*** *No justice, no peace!*]

[***Archive clip, woman:*** *This is ridiculous! Get off of him!*]

[***News clip:*** *Cities from coast to coast have seen protests of outrage and anger over George Floyd's death.*]

SO: In Mississippi, like everywhere, people hit the streets, and the chants....

[***Archive clip, crowd:*** *Black lives matter! Black lives matter!*]

SO: ... of Black lives matter, morphed seamlessly into....

[***Archive clip, crowd:*** *Take it down! Take it down!*]

SO: ... take it down.

[*News clip:* Protesters here in Jackson rallied in front of the governor's mansion.]

[*Archive clip,* **woman:** Peace is love. The Confederate emblem flying in my state flag.]

[*News clip:* Along with calls for an end to police brutality were citizens calling for changes to our state symbol.]

[*Archive clip,* **woman:** Tear it down!]

[*News clip:* Governor Tate Reeves says. . . .]

[*Archive clip,* **Tate Reeves:** The people of Mississippi made a decision in 2001, an overwhelming decision to maintain the flag.]

[*Archive clip,* **woman:** Black lives matter!]

[*News clip:* He's not planning to take any individual action to take it down.]

SO: Cut to the Mississippi State House of Representatives. Representative Chris Bell. . . .

Chris Bell: I represent House District 65 in Jackson.

SO: . . . was between sessions.

CB: A Republican legislator and I actually passed each other in the hallway on my way to grab some coffee. And she made the statement, "Look, if you guys are working on trying to get this flag removed, I will be able to help out behind the scenes." And I said, "Hey, great." And we started the ball rolling.

Shanda Yates: It's time for us to do something now.

SO: Soon Chris and seven other legislators, including Shanda Yates. . . .

SY: Representative, District 64.

SO: Meet in a back room to work up a bill.

SY: We are at a point in the legislature though, where the deadline to introduce general bills was months ago.

SO: The timing of this was such that, in just a few weeks, the entire state capital was all about to go on break for the year.

SY: So for this to happen now, we would have to suspend the rules, which requires a two-thirds vote. Two-thirds of the House of Representatives and two-thirds of the senators have to vote to allow the rules to be suspended.

SO: Mathematically crazy odds.

SY: But I was vocal about it that, yeah, I think we are finally starting to see a shift to get this changed.

SO: So the group sets out to whip some votes, but before they're able to gather even a little bit of momentum their plans leak and an article hits the press.

SY: Saying that, "Hey, Representatives are meeting about this and they're gonna try to change the flag." Oh! So the initial media leak was probably untimely.

SO: Immediately there was push back.

SY: And those representatives that live in rural areas started hearing from their constituents.

[*Phone rings*]

Ken Morgan: Hello?

SO: Hi, Representative Morgan?

KM: Yes.

SO: This is Representative Ken Morgan, Republican. He represents a rural area in southern Mississippi.

Your constituents, what is their voice?

KM: About 74 percent to leave it like it is. I just stopped at a convenience store on my way home and four people in there told me these very words, "Don't let them change our flag."

SO: Wow! Dang.

[*Phone rings*]

Chris McDaniel: This is Chris.

SO: Hi Chris, this is Shima.

CM: Hey, how are ya?

SO: I also spoke with Senator Chris McDaniel. He's been one of the most outspoken critics of changing the flag.

CM: You know, it's funny. It's not really about a flag to me. It's about a philosophical position. When we're talking about monuments, flags, which of course translates into history, and we have one side of this debate, the left, who have become increasingly intolerant of diverse viewpoints, increasingly intolerant of other people's opinions. From my perspective, the price we pay to live in a free society is to occasionally be offended. Diversity of viewpoints matters. Speech matters, expression matters. Their side of the equation doesn't share that opinion any longer. They want uniformity. They want doctrinal truth. And they are just as guilty of being so blind to diversity that they basically quell it at every turn. I think this is a fight philosophically for the future of the country. It's not simply about a flag. It's a position, a mental position. And that's why I think a referendum process would be so important. When you have a referendum, the people are forced into a discussion of the issues.

SO: There he expressed the default Republican position: If you want to change the flag, send it to a vote. That's what we did in 2001 and that's what we should do now.

Does that mean in the Constitution Committee you think that the bill will be, like, just killed there?

CM: Oh yeah. It's already dead.

SO: Oh, really?

CM: I think it's—I think the bill's already dead.

SO: Turns out just a few days after the bill was introduced, what happened behind the scenes....

[*Phone rings*]

Robert Johnson: Hello?

SO: And I learned this from another representative....

RJ: Robert L. Johnson III, Representative of District 94.

SO: ... is that the Lieutenant Governor, Delbert Hosemann, a conservative, did the thing that always happens, the thing that's been happening in one form or another for 120 years. He diverted the baby flag bill to a hostile committee.

RJ: He sent it to a committee that is loaded with ultraconservative Republicans. I mean, at the end of the day, the flag passing or not passing is gonna turn on whether or not Republicans finally wake up and decide this is something we need to do. Can you just hold on a second? I'm picking my mother up.

SO: And just like that, poof.

LS: There was one day last week where I was like, "Holy shit, this is gonna happen." And then the very next day I was like, "Fuck, it's over."

SO: Laurin and I spoke on the phone that day. She was unusually bitter.

LS: But I think it's going to be kind of a hell-to-pay situation because white people here have been so fucking horrible for so fucking long.

SO: We talked for a while, as protests raged outside of my window in Brooklyn and hers in Jackson, Mississippi. I told her about something I'd heard in one of my interviews, that maybe the only way the flag will ever come down in Mississippi is if what happened in South Carolina....

[***News clip:*** *Top lawmakers there now joining the chorus calling for it to be removed after last week's shootings at that historic Black church.*]

SO: ... happens there.

LS: I'm horrified at the thought that there's got to be a murder for this. We've had so many. You know, it's just like—I mean, I don't want somebody to have to—I mean, this is crazy that we're having this discussion. No! No!

SO: Eight days before the end of the legislative session that's where things stood. Nothing was happening and nothing was gonna happen.

LS: Basically what people wanna do is run out the clock.

SO: But then June 18.

[***News clip:*** *We begin with breaking news.*]

[***News clip:*** *Breaking news.*]

[***News clip:*** *The SEC is considering withholding title games tonight amid the ongoing flag fight in the state.*]

SO: Enter the mighty voice of college sports.

[*Archive clip, man:* The SEC—Southeastern Conference—has made it clear. Unless Mississippi takes the Confederate flag off of its state flag, there will be no SEC championships taking place on any campus in Mississippi. That is essentially a divestment practice.]

SO: Suddenly, the flag debate was on a whole new level.

[*Archive clip, man:* I keep telling people, if you want to affect America, you must deal with money.]

SO: One day later. . . .

[*News clip:* The NCAA announced it is expanding its Confederate flag policy. . . .]

SO: The big dog steps in.

[*News clip:* . . . banning all championship events from being held in states where the Confederate flag is flown. Mississippi is the only state affected.]

SO: From there, a cascade of businesses threaten to divest in rapid succession. First it was Sanderson Farms. 15,000 employees. Then. . . .

[*News clip:* Walmart says it will no longer have the Mississippi state flag in its stores.]

SO: . . . Walmart. Twenty-three thousand employees. Same day. . . .

[*News clip:* The Mississippi Baptist Convention said something similar.]

SO: The Mississippi Baptist Convention, more than half a million members. . . .

[*Archive clip, man:* In light of our understanding of his teaching, Jesus Christ.]

[*Archive clip, man:* I am compelled to urge the legislature to change our state flag.]

[*Phone rings*]

LS: That's you?

SO: I hop on the phone with Laurin to review this new progress.

LS: There's a statement that I can forward you that our lieutenant governor just released.

SO: Here's the thing. I talked to a senator today who said they're ten votes away.

LS: Oh, God.

SO: She showed me tweets of her flag waving at BLM protests. And then we talked about all the businesses that have just put up her flag in the past few days.

LS: Whitney Bank, which is a big presence on the coast, is putting up a Stennis banner as soon as it gets back from the printer. And this huge

Gothic fabulous—I think it's the tallest building downtown—the Lamar Life building in Jackson, they need a ten by fifteen flag. So we had to order it.

SO: Outside of the NBC headquarters, there's a flag of yours.

LS: [*Gasps*]

SO: Did you see that?

LS: Will you take a picture of that? No!

SO: Two days to the deadline. . . .

CB: You had a couple of legislators who have come out on the right side of history.

SY: It's very close right now.

SO: Chris Bell and Shanda Yates tell me that they've inched forward just a little bit.

CB: We're hoping that the momentum will grow over the weekend.

[*Phone rings*]

Chris McDaniel's Voicemail: Hey, this is Chris. I'm sorry I couldn't answer the phone.

SO: Also tried Senator Chris McDaniel a few times.

CMV: Just leave a message and I'll get right back to you. The mailbox is full. Goodbye.

[**News clip:** *Momentum is building to change Mississippi's state flag, even as the legislative session winds down.*]

[**News clip:** *The House Democratic minority leaders say they are about one to two votes away from getting some movement going.*]

SO: Around this time, with Team Change still a few votes short and just a few days left to the deadline. . . .

CB: The Republicans brought out the two-flag option.

SY: There's been an idea floated about adopting a second coequal flag. Keep our current flag and also have a new flag. Kind of separate but equal flags.

CB: That's not even—that's not up for debate.

SY: It's a weird idea for me to wrap my head around.

SO: On the eve of the deadline, it seemed like things had suddenly stalled. Suddenly, all the senators weren't returning my calls. Meanwhile, Laurin was getting attacked online. A few members of the Mississippi Black Lives Matter movement started publicly saying that the new flag should be designed by a Black person and should not bear the name of a segregationist.

LS: Well, I—I met with some folks who are with Black Lives Matter and it was really helpful to realize in person in dialogue, how much of a roadblock the association, or even just the perceived association with my grandfather was. I mean, you have to kind of realize how hard this is to happen in Mississippi. And it's kind of absurd and crazy, but all the planets were aligning. And then all of a sudden, it became—my last name became this huge issue and I'm like, "Well, I'm getting the hell out of the way, because this needs to happen."

SO: She ended up posting a statement online.

SO: Can you read it to me?

LS: Yes. "Dear friends, Mississippi will soon know all the benefits and joy that come with having a state flag that is evocative, not provocative. Working hard for six years toward that goal has been one of the best experiences of my life. In a continued effort to be of service, I'll be stepping away from this endeavor, as I understand the hurt and potential harm my last name can cause, but I will always continue to fight for Mississippi and her people, which I consider both a duty and a joy. Mississippi needs and deserves a new flag. Help make it so. Laurin."

SO: That's kind of—that's heartbreaking.

LS: No, it's—it's good. It's all right.

[*News clip:* Breaking this morning, Laurin Stennis the creator of a popular alternative to the state flag says she's stepping away from her endeavor. Her grandfather was US Senator John Stennis, who served Mississippi on Capitol Hill for 41 years. He was also. . . .]

[*Senate tape:* House come to order. Please stand as we're led in prayer today by guest minister to be introduced by the lady from Harrison. Remain standing there for the pledge.]

JA: Saturday June 27, 2020.

[*Senate tape:* Thank you, Mr. Speaker. Thank you, ladies and gentlemen.]

JA: State legislators finally meet to vote on the flag.

SO: Minutes before, I got a series of frantic texts from Shanda Yates. "Shima, it's now." "Looks like it's not happening." "It's on." "Honestly have no idea."

[*Senate tape:* Thank you father for Mississippi.]

JA: Session begins with a prayer.

[*Senate tape:* We ask you and beseech you that you would be in their hearts, that what is in their heart will transfer to their mind. That they may do the things that are pleasing unto God for the good of all Mississippians and even our country. Forgive us of our sins we pray. Amen.]

JA: Then. . . .

[*Senate tape:* Pledge, please.]

JA: ... appropriately enough. ...

[**Senate tape:** *I pledge allegiance to the flag of the United States of America.*]

JA: ... everybody faces a big American flag. Next to it, the 1894 Mississippi state flag—the Confederate one. And they pledge their allegiance. Maybe for the last time. Maybe not.

[**Senate tape:** *Open the machine, Madame Clerk.*]

SO: In the audience, you can see a few Black representatives are wearing masks. One has the words "Take It Down" written on his. And another has the number 846 printed on his.

[**Senate tape:** *House come back to order.*]

JA: After that, speeches.

[**Senate tape:** *I rise before you today in this chamber. The eyes of our state, the nation and indeed the world, are on this House this morning.*]

JA: The tenor of the speeches reminded me of reading John and Abigail Adams's letters. How they would write in this way where they knew that we would be reading their letters hundreds of years later.

[**Senate tape:** *History will be made here today.*]

[**Senate tape:** *I will know exactly where I was on this day.*]

JA: There was that same awareness here.

[**Senate tape:** *Woke up this morning like many of you and I watched the news. And on each channel they were talking about the vote on Mississippi's flag. That's on national news. The international news is there too. It is so because of what that flag stands for.*]

JA: You had a few minutes of debate.

[**Senate tape:** *We want to take the joy away from them.*]

JA: ... where you heard the arguments.

[**Senate tape:** *We as a body want to take that from them.*]

[**Senate tape:** *I appreciate your position. That is not the position of this body here today.*]

SO: At times, during these debates. ...

[**Senate tape:** *And I understand that.*]

[**Senate tape:** *Good.*]

[**Senate tape:** *My. ...*]

SO: Things got a little testy.

[**Senate tape:** *And I'm not trying to be argumentative with you.*]

[**Senate tape:** *Me either. Me either. Me either.*]

[**Archive clip, Senator Chris McDaniel:** *I remember watching. ...*]

SO: Senator Chris McDaniel.

[*Archive clip, SCM:* . . . the American flag being burned. That really bothered me. I didn't understand why someone would do something like that. The symbol seemed so pure, so innocent. And so I asked my father, I said, "Why are they burning this flag?" And he said, "Well son, it's complicated."]

SO: His closing shot was a story about his dad, how his dad taught him that flags, just like the people they represent, are complicated and we should embrace that, not erase it.

[*Senate tape:* This is a tough decision. It's a very tough decision. I know it's tough. It's hard. But this is why you're elected to be in these positions.]

JA: After that. . . .

[*Senate tape:* So now Senator, we have a motion. Can you do the morning roll call?]

JA: The moment of truth.

[*Senate tape:* Motion to use the morning roll call. Does anyone object to the procedure?]

JA: Now to be honest, there are actually two votes: one in the House and the Senate. We're gonna focus in on the Senate. That's what you're hearing because that's the vote that really counts.

[*Senate tape:* Roll call. Is that what your motion is?]

JA: If you recall, they needed a two-thirds majority to suspend the rules in order to move forward. If they get that majority, it's effectively a vote to change the flag. Which means they need thirty-five out of fifty-two votes.

[*Senate tape:* Mr. Clerk.]

[*Senate tape:* Barnett, Blackmon, Blackwell, Blount, Boyd, Branning, Bryan, Butler, Carter]

SO: The clerk calls the fifty senators one by one. They do a voice vote.

[*Senate tape:* Simmons of the twelfth. Simmons of the thirteenth. Sojourner. Sparks.]

SO: Then he reads the tally. First the yeas.

[*Senate tape:* Voting "yes" or "yea." Barnett, Blackman, Blackwell, Blount, Boyd, Bryan, Butler, Carter, DeBar, DeLano, Doty, England, Frazier, Harkins, Hopson, Horhn, Jackson of the fifteenth, Jackson of the eleventh, Jackson of the thirty-second.]

SO: Then the nays.

[*Senate tape:* Voting "no" or "nay." Branning, Caughman, Chassaniol, Chism, Fillingane, Hill, Johnson, McCaughn, McDaniel, McLendon, Seymour, Sojourner, Sparks, Suber and Whaley.]

JA: Then there is a two-minute silence where it seems like there are some recounts. Again, they need to get to thirty-five out of fifty-two votes.

Watching this on the stream at this point, I'm thinking if there are these recounts that probably means they don't have it.

[**Senate tape:** *By a vote of thirty-six to fourteen, the motion passes.*]

[*Applause*]

[**Senate tape:** *Mr. President, I ask for immediate release.*]

[**Senate tape:** *Seeing no objection, immediate release is granted.*]

JA: For 126 years, the Mississippi state flag had the Confederate flag on it. But no longer.

SO: Just watched it.

SY: Yes! Yes!

SO: Shanda Yates.

SY: The old flag is gone.

RJ: All the hard work has paid off.

SO: Robert Johnson.

RJ: The people get to see Mississippi for who they really are.

CB: It was a victory for all of us.

SO: Chris Bell.

CB: Mississippi is ready to enter the global market.

KM: Hell, what can you say? I voted not to change it. I mean. . . .

SO: Ken Morgan.

KM: That's all I can do.

SO: Oh my gosh. Did you watch?

JH: I did. I saw it.

SO: And John Hawkins, where it all began.

JH: I was watching it with my son, my eighteen-year-old son who's headed to the University of Kentucky in the fall. But I'm not sure he fully understood the gravity of the moment.

SO: John has hinted to us that he might now finally move back to Mississippi, and perhaps politics will be in his future.

JA: Now as for how they got the vote, because remember they came into the day a few votes shy. Turns out the thing that pushed them over the edge was quite literally God. At the very last minute, a few Republicans agreed to vote to remove the old flag only if the new flag had the words "In God We Trust" on it.

SO: Do you know where that came from?

RJ: Well—well, we still live in a conservative state and part of—part of what it took to get people to cross that line of voting to take the Confederate flag down is to give them some alternative that they could go sell to the traditionalists out there and they want that on their flag.

JA: Seeing the way it all played out, was that bittersweet from your perspective?

LS: I think that's a good way to put it. Yeah. Yeah. But you know, wow! We got—we got the current flag down, the 1894 flag down. And so have been celebrating that for sure.

JA: A few days later, Governor Tate Reeves, he of the blackface battle flag-loving fraternity, signed the bill into law.

[*News clip:* It is an amazing, historical moment to be witnessing this: the last time the Mississippi state flag raised at the Mississippi state capitol now lowered, never to be raised again.]

SO: And then all 1894 flags were officially removed from all State buildings.

LS: But you know, in true fashion we've made the replacement the most complicated procedure ever.

JA: Yeah.

[*News clip:* Of course the process now as they do this, they now—they soon—the nine-member commission who will be tasked with the process of finding a flag design.]

JA: For the moment Mississippi, which used to be the only state in the union with the Confederate battle flag on it is now the only state in the union without a flag at all.

KL: And I just think it's amazing that—that Mississippians did something radical. It's radical to be a state without a flag. You know what I'm saying? Like, that's—that's not like—it's radical to be like, "You know what? We don't have a fucking flag right now, so we're gonna have to build some shit together." This is the beginning. This ain't the end. But right now, I'm not gonna think about that. Right now I'm just gonna be happy. I'm gonna be really happy for this weekend. That's something I never thought I would see happen. Something my granny never thought would see happen, you know? So it's not the end, but it's a victory. And I think going forward, like, my utopia would be like that Laurin and a lot of other brilliant, thoughtful, loving people were central to the design of the new flag. Like, you know, how do we share and do right by the best of Mississippi? The best of Mississippi.

JA: Two quick postscripts. From what we understand, orders of the Confederate flag have apparently shot through the roof in Mississippi. And second, just this week in the wake of the flag proceedings we learned that twenty-six legislators have tested positive for COVID. This episode was brought to you through a collaboration between OSM Audio and *Radiolab*. It was produced and reported by Shima Oliaee with production assistance from Annie McEwen and Bethel Habte. Thanks also to Kiese Laymon, author of *Heavy*, a great memoir. Definitely recommend. To Tad Davis, Ray Hawkins, Rory Doyle, Katie McKee, Adam Gunshow, Kayleigh Skinner, Giacomo Bologna, Luke Ramseth and Sarah Fowler. I'm Jad Abumrad. Thanks for listening.

On Resilience, Tender Rituals, and Responsible Love: Talking with Kiese Laymon

April Pejic / 2021

From *The Rumpus*, March 15, 2021. Reprinted with permission.

I read the revised collection while caring for my own grandmother as she recovered from surgery, which is perhaps why Grandmama's strength and wisdom on the page, and Laymon's connection with her, felt like such a balm to the isolation and anxiety I was experiencing. I had the opportunity to sit down with Laymon over Zoom to discuss *How to Slowly Kill Yourself and Others*, the pandemic raging around us, and, most importantly, our grandmamas.

The Rumpus: You write so beautifully in the new introduction to *How to Slowly Kill Yourself and Others in America* and in "You Are the Second Person" about the painful experience with the initial predatory publisher of the book. In some ways, it feels like all the essays speak to that process. What drove that decision, and was there healing for you in revision?

Kiese Laymon: There is a desperation in that book. I was desperately trying to find someone to collaborate on art with. That's it. I needed help. And publishing in this nation mostly said no. So, all the pieces are sort of rooted in that experience of asking folks who actually need your help more than you need theirs to help you. It messed with my head, and revising the book helped me begin healing from all of those publishing experiences. It also reminded me that though my experience is specifically shaped, its consistency is the same as what happens to humans. We beg for help from folks who need our help more than we need theirs.

Rumpus: Reading through the book, I noticed an interesting language choice. You write, "This is our book," or "This is our house." There's a very communal idea of ownership that runs through your work and seems to apply to your entire family.

Laymon: Yeah, I do that intentionally. I mean because one, it's what I feel. And that "our" is so rooted in my grandmother. Anytime I use "our" I'm talking about her. Sometimes I use "our" when I'm trying to make big claims about the nation or just people, and it's hard to make those proclamations in writing and have them land. Usually when I say "our," I'm talking about the family my grandma built. I think it's important for those of us who write and use the "I" so much to remember we are still a part of a family.

Rumpus: It is so important. I feel like there's all this attention to individualism. We're losing what it means to be a part of a collective and a collective identity.

Laymon: Stuff like this pandemic is supposed to be what helps us remember just on a basic level. Like, I didn't really understand school spirit. I mean, I did coming up in Jackson because we had Jackson State, but that was city spirit, and we were hype about our city. But I went to Indiana for grad school and there is school spirit, but it's really all about how much Indiana hates Michigan and Purdue. Theoretically, this pandemic should have connected everyone because we're all literally in the world to varying degrees because of power and negligence, we're all trying to fight something we've never fought before. We've all been affected by this. Somebody we know, somebody we love, somebody we taught, somebody who taught us. If there's any time for communal anything, it's now, right? We can love one another, hold ourselves accountable, be tender, and try to make it better, try to examine what led us to this place and make it better going forward. That's what should bring us together.

Rumpus: From what I've read of your work, our lives have a number of parallels. There have to be more people like us who got a lot of their raising from their grandmamas. Nobody really ever talks about that or talks about the work women of that generation have done.

Laymon: Oh yeah. I love talking about grandmamas. Probably too much. I'm writing my next book about my grandmama.

Rumpus: That's awesome. What are you working on?

Laymon: It's a book called *Good God*, and it's about intimacy and forgiveness which I've been thinking a lot about during this pandemic. My great-grandfather abandoned my grandmother and his family when my grandmother was four and came back to her when she was fifty-two. I was staying with her at the time. He was there for seven days and at the end of those seven days, he died. He came back to her to die. I didn't know that at the time. I had never known about him. I just remember that I had never seen her look at anyone with, it's more than hate. It's more than resentment. There was obviously so much sadness, but she was so mad at him. When he knocked on the screen door, I had never seen her look like that at someone, just disgusted. But she took him in, and ultimately, she forgave him. She forgave him, but she also picked on him. My grandma is virtuous and all that, but she can also be a little raw. A little rough.

Rumpus: Yes. My grandmother will hold a grudge like it is her job. It's both beautiful to behold and frightening.

Laymon: It is frightening because it shakes a familiar perception of my grandmama, of her kindness and generosity. And she is those things, but just like everybody, she can pick on people. I pay for her healthcare, and for the first five years, she just ran through healthcare providers, because she would say things to hurt their feelings. Like, "Kie, they over here trying to cook, but you can't call that cooking." My granny is so interesting because she won't ask for help, but she will accept it. But when she needs to ask for help, she is afraid to. Part of growing up in poverty in the South, you didn't go to hospitals or doctors. Instead they'd come up with some old weird concoction at home. My granny has diabetes, and she got this big sore on her foot. She packed it with some home remedy, but it got infected. My mom kept smelling something, and Grandmama knew it was her foot, but she wouldn't say anything because at that point she was ashamed. For me to see my grandmother feel ashamed is the hardest thing. That is one of the things that's pushed me to try to be a decent writer and work is because I don't want her to be ashamed of me. I think everybody needs someone that they don't want to let down or shame. I feel for those people who don't have anybody who loves them right, who they're afraid to let down.

Rumpus: It's interesting that you bring that up. In "Hey Mama: An Essay in Emails," there is a lot of indirect discussion about shame that seems to be absent from the writing you do about your grandmother.

Laymon: That's true. Man, I never thought about that before. This new thing that I'm writing is all about that. You know, I feel closer to my grandmama but in reality I'm much more close to my mom. There's an intimacy with my mother that is different with my grandma. I think I'm afraid to break a shrouded image I have of her, if I write too much about her relationship to shame.

Rumpus: You have written a lot about your grandmother and work. It seems like she has worked as a form of love. I want to hear about her art.

Laymon: She's known for being a hard worker, but she's really known for being a good seamstress. My grandmother was the only one in her family who stayed in Mississippi. She didn't go up North like her sisters and brothers. When my grandmother was nine, she went to stay with a woman who was fifteen years old. She took my grandmother in and helped her. But then my grandma's father ended up getting this woman pregnant. Anyway, my grandmother would ask her relatives in the Midwest for clothes they didn't want anymore, and she would bring them back to Forest, Mississippi. And she would use the patterns to make clothes for her kids. They were always the best clothes. And to this day, I had to buy my grandma a shed just so she'd have a place to put all her church dresses because she never wants to wear a church dress twice. This woman has a whole country work shed filled with, to me, gaudy clothes. Lots of red, shiny black, and shiny white, and she'd have a matching hat, matching earrings, and matching shoes. She was always dressed to the T, but if somebody wore something like hers, she'd be so tight. She'd be so upset that she couldn't be singularly stylish that day.

Rumpus: My grandmother is like that, too. Appearance has always been important to her, but also the appearance of not trying.

Laymon: Yes, yes. Grandmama extends that to everything. She's a hard worker, but she's much more interested in being a beautiful worker who appears not to work hard, not to try hard. But that's the thing about appearance. You don't just wake up like that. You know what I mean?

Rumpus: Right. I wonder where that pressure comes from.

Laymon: And how much of it is conventions of femininity or how much of it is regional. Yeah, because acting like it is natural is so cool. That's the epitome of cool, right? That's what cool actually is; I woke up like this. That's the whole point: I want you to think I woke up like this, even though you know there's no way. But also I think it's something to be comfortable in those clothes. If you put nice clothes on me, I'm not going to look right. I think there's something about just the comfort it takes to be adorned like that and look comfortable in that kind of outfit. Because all of us don't have that.

Rumpus: That's a good point. Speaking of that, I watched the book launch zoom for *How to Slowly Kill Yourself and Others in America* that you did with your Aunt Sue. That was such a beautiful, beautiful moment to see the two of you together talking. I'm not personally a believer, but she made me believe.

Laymon: That's what I really want to talk about because I'm not [a believer] either, in that traditional sense, but I believe in the practice. I believe that the practice can save people. Do you know what I mean? I think holy practices, and belief in something, can save people. The practices that sustained my grandmother were all rooted in sisterhood and the women in her community. I think that's really important for me to remember.

Rumpus: Your aunt said, "We're overcomers because of our testimonies. Your testimony is your life." That's so beautiful.

Laymon: Yeah, I believe that. I wouldn't use that language, that we all witness. But to use my words, it means to write about it and to create art around what we witnessed. To use her words, it'd be to testify about what you witnessed. But to me, witnessing is about making art, talking, putting words together. It's an attempt at art, at full assemblage to make meaning. So I believe you got to testify, but what do we do with those things that we're scared to talk about because we don't want them to be true?

Rumpus: In "Quick Feet," you write, "Grandmama and I love talking about words. She was better than anyone I'd ever known at bending, breaking, and building words that weren't in the dictionary." What were some of her words?

Laymon: There's a tradition that she comes from, but also just the Bible. We don't talk about the Bible a lot, but there's just so many words and turns of phrase in that book. Like "starnated fool." She'd say, "You acting like a starnated fool." She also always talks about this phrase in the book, "You know, God gave you five senses for a reason. If you don't use them, you the biggest fool in the world." That one speaks to her warning personality. She's always saying you got everything you need, if you just listen and you just accept. So it's almost a way of blaming yourself if it goes wrong.

Rumpus: I've seen my grandmother almost beat herself up about not knowing the future. Like it's easier to tell yourself that you could have been prepared for something than to be upset about what's happened.

Laymon: I think with that generation, and this could be reductive, but there's a particular kind of toughness that the world required. And I'm not just saying that in a positive way. I think that toughness obviously led to people not being in tune with different emotional registers. But the thing about my grandmama that's so strange to me: she is no doubt the toughest person I have ever known, but the rituals that she created were tender rituals. Like when she had home mission and she had those women coming to the house and they would talk, they would try to be their own therapists, which is not healthy, but there weren't many people welcoming working-class Black women into a therapist office back then. They didn't have the money to go, anyway. Sometimes it seems like the people who are most resilient have a hard time with the details, the finer points of love in life. One of the reasons I'm so indebted to her is because of her toughness and her tenderness. She modeled both.

Rumpus: You state in "Author's Note #2": "All the pieces in this book are differently shaped, paced, and greased with orange-red odes to my grandmama and her generation of Black women in Mississippi." Why is paying tribute to these women so important for you?

Laymon: Honestly, because they have never been given what they deserved from anyone other than themselves. I don't want to emulate what this nation does to Black women of that generation. I want to serve and share with and build on the legacies of my grandmother and her generation of Black women.

Rumpus: So you started the Catherine Coleman Literary Arts and Justice Program.

Laymon: Yeah, my grandmama didn't finish school because she had my uncle so young and had to work. She worked at a chicken plant and as a domestic in white homes. She had to go back and get her GED, so reading and writing were always crucial to her. She couldn't go to school, but all of her kids went and all of her kids became some kind of teacher. Even my Uncle Jimmy was a Sunday school teacher. I'm a teacher, my cousins, my aunt Linda, my mother. Teachers are so overloaded that they can't teach creative writing, so we created a mechanism where kids who are interested and their parents can take creative writing workshops taught by our current [University of Mississippi] students and have readings in the communities where these kids and their parents are. We would also invite the kids and their parents to come to the University of Mississippi because a lot of those kids have never been to the university, and a lot of our grad students haven't been to different parts of the state. So, it was one way to connect people and encourage imagination and empathy through reading, writing, revising and sharing. My grandmama, she never made no serious money ever, but she saved a lot, and she would give whatever she could, whether it was the kids from the trailer park next door or her own kids with graduate degrees who were in trouble. That's what I'm saying in terms of responsible love. She gave us the best model of how to be and she never tried to hurt us.

"Conjuring Love": A Conversation with Kiese Laymon

Jane Ratcliffe / 2021

From *The Los Angeles Review of Books*, July 13, 2021. Reprinted with permission.

Jane Ratcliffe: How difficult is it for you to write about racism?

Kiese Laymon: Nobody ever asked that question. I need to write about it so I can feel stable. But it's sort of terrifying to write through what we have done with this idea of race in this world, but definitely in this nation. I try to sometimes lean into the absurdity of it because that's how I can get through it. I need to laugh through parts of it. But I'm always crying through it. Because it's all just sort of terrifying.

JR: In keeping with this, your characters tend to speak very plainly, very frankly, and by doing so the truth of the world is revealed. And sometimes that truth is simultaneously horrifying and ridiculous. For instance, when describing Klansmen, City says, "I didn't know if Mama Lara had ever been beaten by a man in a sheet." You have so many sentences like this that just state the basic facts. This is a grown man walking around with a sheet over him. . . .

KL: . . . with a sheet and two eyeholes. . . .

JR: . . . which is ridiculous, but he's also very dangerous.

KL: Mississippi is just packed with absurdity. Starting with the colors: you have this big field of beautiful white cotton. And then you have these Black human beings initially that have to pick it. That's fucking weird. Visually, that's weird. And then you have these groups of people over here who might be land-owning who decide at night that they're going to put on fucking sheets and ride horses and terrorize people who don't have a fraction of what the fuck they have. If you don't find the absurdity in it, you go crazy, because it's so brutal, it's so terrifying, but it's also just nuts. They're wearing motherfucking sheets and they're burning crosses for people who would never do that to them. Sometimes we forget to just describe the shit in front of us. We can't get lost in the grinding absurdity of it all. But it's absurd. It's absurd that my grandmama couldn't piss in the same bathroom as your mom. It doesn't matter if they're great people or shitty people. They can't piss in the same bathroom. It's absurd and terrifying. And I'm not going to let these people not allow me to laugh at shit. Just because they're so fucking cruel. I'm going to have to laugh at it to write through it, because if I don't, I don't know how to get into it.

JR: Agreed. City becomes an internet sensation for shouting "And fuck white folks!" when given the word "n----rdly" in the contest "Can You Use That Word in a Sentence?" Later he reflects on not knowing "if there was a difference between being right and doing wrong." Is there a "right" way to fight white supremacy?

KL: That is a great question. I'm scared to answer that either way. I don't know if there's a right way, but I think that, if you fight white supremacy by yourself, you're going to die brutally. If we fight white supremacy collectively, we give ourselves more of a chance. But the problem is that we don't walk through as collectives, right? At some point, you got to go to sleep and you got to wake up, you got to use the bathroom. So that's the hard part. The wrong way to fight this shit is individually; the right way to fight it is collectively, with folks who love you. But you can't always be with your people. And white supremacy never fucking stops. That's the thing. It gets you when you sleep. It gets you right when you wake up. It gets you right before you go to sleep. I feel for anyone who has to fight that shit alone. And at different times we all do. And that's the scary part.

JR: *Long Division* takes place in Mississippi. I know you have deep affection for Mississippi, but given the state of America, do you ever fanaticize about living elsewhere?

KL: I think about leaving Mississippi every single day. Right now, what I'm thinking about is how you can be of the most use and service to a space and place. I'm not sure if that necessarily means you have to live there. It might. I used to think it definitely meant that you needed to be there. But I don't know if I can be there and be healthy. So, it might mean that I go live somewhere else and just find ways to be of most use to Mississippi. There's no way I'm going to be living in Mississippi for the rest of my life.

JR: It can be hard to find a balance when you want to do what's right and good, but then what toll does that take on you? Where do you put yourself on the care spectrum?

KL: I thought a lot about that this year with COVID-19. Because, early in it, I was just like, "Oh my lord, I wish I had a kid; I wish I had a pet; I wish I had something." I was like, "Oh, this is one of the reasons people have all of these markers of adulthood because it's sort of hard to keep living sometimes when you don't have a partner, a kid, someone that depends on you." I thought a lot about what it meant to live in Mississippi as a Black man, alone, at forty-six. That's some shit I never read about. That Black guy who lives in Mississippi, who can live anywhere in the world, who lives in Mississippi, alone. I was like, "Oh fuck, I have to write this because nobody else has written it." But I'm too weak to write this right now. I'm trying to do that now. But that's a hard, sad thing. Right?

JR: Yes, loneliness can be staggering. Sadness also seems to be a problem for your characters. City's base essence is sorrow, though he does his best to keep it hidden. In fact, all your characters carry tremendous sorrow. Do you think at our base, we're all sad?

KL: I do believe that. I don't like to be that person who says blanket shit about all humans, because there's going to be outliers, but I don't know how our base essences can't be sadness, given what we've done.

Whether or not we consciously are taking inventory, we know what we've done. And we know what we're doing. Like, I know what our being on this computer using electricity is doing for other parts of the world. And I love communicating like this. But the things that we love in this culture, the things that bring us pleasure, often are being done at the expense of other people. And that shit is not good.

I think some part of us knows that and wants to remedy it. Just because sadness might be a baseline, it doesn't mean that it's forever. We can play that baseline a whole lot of different ways. That's one of the reasons that keeps me believing and loving people generally. I think, at the core, none of us have been given a fair shot. None of us. Look at Trump. People think you're supposed to have two parents, you're supposed to go to Ivy League schools and go to the private schools and all that bullshit and have all the money. Look at that fucking dude, that motherfucker's burning from the inside out. Right? All of us have been given a fucked-up hand. Some people have been given worse hands and are kinder, in spite of that. Some people aren't.

I first started writing *Long Division* when Bush was doing all the war crimes and people were talking about torture and I was like, "What the fuck would I do to George Bush?" I wrote this long piece that was all about how I would rehabilitate George Bush. *Long Division*, in part, is about, how do you rehabilitate people who harm you? And should you? What happens when there's years and centuries and decades of what the grandmother goes through in that book? And I'm not sure. I don't want fucking Trump to go to prison, because I don't believe in prison. But what do I want? What would happen if he had to drink cranberry juice and listen to Toni Morrison's short stories? But that's how that book was actually born. I was starting to think about alternatives to incarceration. What do you do to rehabilitate people? Or can you?

JR: Did you come to a conclusion?

KL: I think you can. That's what I'm saying, that book is all about education. When those Freedom Rider folks came to Mississippi, they had the right idea. There's a critique from Mississippians that some of them were patronizing, but they had the right idea pedagogically. Everything from cops to militarism, to all of that shit, is rooted in education. A radical upheaval in education in this world changes everything. That means we have to change the way teachers are not just paid but also taught. We have to destroy prisons and make schools that really take care and love the people that need it the most. I think it's there. But so much has to be extracted now, because it's tied up in so much money. But there's a way to be better. There's a way to be kinder, there's a way to be more tender.

JR: In part, this book is about City trying to save his grandfather. Yet he also questions: "In real life, do we really need our granddaddies?" And he is surrounded by women, as are most of your characters. What role do you see men playing in a healthy, thriving society? How about women?

KL: I think kids just need waves of multifaceted love, and I don't think it matters what package that love comes in. So, I don't think we need men or women, we need people who are willing to ask themselves questions with the intent to grow and grow backward accounting for things that we've done. And that way, I don't think it matters if they're genderqueer, if they're men, if they're women, but in my state, in my family, it was just all women. My grandfather drowned. My uncle was around, he died in 2007, and I didn't grow up with my father. Most of the families I know down south, the women are carrying an unfair burden in those relationships. But at the same time, I'm not one of those people who's going be like, we need present Black men. I think we need loving people.

JR: What are some of the questions that you would encourage people to ask?

KL: We always have to be asking ourselves, when do we most want to be a man? And when do we least want to be a man? What parts of masculinity do we not want to be true about us that actually are true? Masculinity encourages a perpetual deception, that once you break it, everything breaks. Which is why people don't want to break it. I think the question of, what do you not want to be true but is likely true about yourself, is a question we should all ask ourselves, every day, more than once. And how does that thing that you don't want to be true impact the way you treat other people?

JR: You write a lot about the body in this book, and in all your work, in terms of race, gender, sexuality, and also as a carrier of often unbearable emotions such as grief, anger, longing. Can you speak about bodies? What is your relationship like with your body these days?

KL: I was in the emergency room two weekends ago because I had some weird growth in the right part of my ribs. Whenever I go, it's just terrible, and I have insurance. I'm a big Black person and I have money, but I don't dress like I have money. So they just don't treat you right. But I also just feel so good that I've given my health over to another person, even if I don't think that person is going to treat me fairly. There's something, sadly, peaceful about that sort of submission. And I find it more so when my body's bigger. When I was really small and had a six-pack and was very compact, I didn't even go to the doctor. I didn't want anybody to see me then. But now, as a much bigger person, it's definitely more terrifying. But also, I feel like, once they stick a needle in my arm or once they do anything, weigh me, I'm just like, alright, fuck it. I'm here. I'm getting help. And there's something freeing in asking for help even if it's from people you don't trust.

JR: Are you okay now? Has the growth gotten smaller?

KL: Yeah, it got smaller. I've gone to the doctor more times in this past year than I've gone probably in my entire life. I feel like I'm psychologically healthier than I've been. But I've got really terrible hip arthritis and that makes it hard for me to do the things I want to. But in a lot of ways, that saves me, too. Because if my hips work, I just never stop running. I'm just going be that fool who runs himself into the dirt, like every time.

JR: If you didn't have the arthritis, do you think you would still be working out?

KL: Yeah. I was down to 149 with hardly any body fat and I was not going to stop. Then my body just broke. And it stopped me. It doesn't hurt too bad, I can deal with the pain, it's the mobility. When you have arthritis, you get to a point where you can't even make a stride. But I also realize that my writing life kind of picked up when I was able to stop running. I've not talked about that before, but I literally had to sit down and not run from that shit on that page. I could tell myself I was running to think through it and work through it, but I was running away from a lot of that stuff. Because I could pat myself on the back for running fifteen, sixteen miles. And then I didn't have to do the writing that I needed to do.

JR: City closes out Book One by saying, "All we needed to know about how to love better in Mississippi was in our hands." And later, Baize says: "My Klan would go town to town with coloring books asking folks who didn't get along to color together." Is this possible? Is love enough to solve all of this?

KL: My problem is, I believe it really is. But I think conjuring love is harder than passing some shit in the fucked-up US Senate. It's harder than getting your community to do whatever the fuck might be best for it in the future. Really putting the needs of yourself in this world and your neighbor ahead of wants that could be destructive. I don't know if that's love, but that's hard. We don't do it. What we do now is we try to do public policy, we try to do activism, we try to do all of these things. We have to do all these things. Love, as Baldwin and Morrison and all these others explored it, is nowhere near as rich. . . . We're nowhere near as loving as we think we are. But I do believe it.

JR: How do you define love?

KL: I think love is that force that individuals, families, communities, groups of people can create. I think love is an energy that we must create to keep us healthy and alive. This is tough. It's too hard a question for Easter.

JR: At one point, Coach is admonishing City to manage the freedom that white people have "allowed" Black people. In response, City says, "They can only do as much harm as you let them, and all y'all oldheads are letting them do way too much." That got me thinking about who is responsible for change. Because older generations keep looking to the younger generation to fix everything. But you know, because you teach, that young folks are riddled with anxiety and depression, especially now. Are we putting too much pressure on them when they're already under pressure?

KL: I love that question because I think we can be of use. A lot of professional, political-class people of older generations, they want younger people to follow them. And often that means following the same rules or strategies and tactics that didn't necessarily work. So, I do think it's okay to let the younger people lead. But that doesn't mean we don't have anything to do. It might mean we have more work to do. But we might have to be collaborative and ask them how we can be of service. Because, yes, they are riddled with anxiety, depression, and all of that, but also, writ large, their ideas for a more just world are better than ours. And ours were better than our parents.' The younger generation of people now are presenting a lot of ideas that are out of the box, but a lot of them are just much more oriented. So, I'm saying we can let them lead. But that doesn't mean we don't have to also be out there working.

JR: Lineage is vitally important to City. And I believe it is to you, too. Why? What do you perceive our ancestors hold that we need? Or is it more a matter of honoring them? If so, why? Some of them were awful people.

KL: That's true. Some of them are awful people, but when I'm looking at Black Americans from the South, you know, awful people galore. But they didn't want to come here. They got stolen. They didn't want to get exploited and then they got exploited. And they didn't want to have children with people that they didn't want to have children with, but that's what happened. And they didn't want to not be able to be married or fucking vote or live wherever the fuck they couldn't live freely. People kept themselves alive partially so you could have a life that was not theirs. People died so I could write, so I'm not going to waste my writing. And people died trying to keep me from writing. White folks killed people because they didn't want me to be able to read and write. So, yes, lots of awful people in our ancestral past. But at least, when you talk about Black folks, they weren't given fair access to healthy choices, second chances. That means something to me.

JR: Beautifully put. After Sooo Sad and his buddies attack City and City's grandma retaliates, Sooo Sad says, "Y'all mad at something more than me. I ain't do it. [. . .] Y'all making this personal." I was struck by the bone-deep truth of this. How do we assess the individual when we each also carry the communal?

KL: We have to want to see the individual and the communal in every person who does us good or harm. So the hardest part of that book was putting shit that actually makes sense in the mouth of that character. Obviously, that character does some things that are terrible. But for that book to work, you have to sort of feel some sympathy for him. I think when that character is like, "You're blaming me for some shit that I didn't do," the book is saying, "I'm blaming you for some shit you didn't stop." And that's very different. Once you look at it that way, that's when you see how all of us have our foot on somebody's neck.

JR: City's mom drills into him that his actions not only affect him but "those yet to be born."

KL: This is the conceit of the book: what we're doing today is going to impact tomorrow in some form or fashion. So maybe we should live today in a way that gives people tomorrow the best chance. That's all. Because I'm talking to you for lots of reasons, but one is because people of Mississippi organized and fought and gave me a chance that other people said I wasn't deserving of. And I think we have to do that going forward. And when we fail, this is as important as any of it, we have to be honest about the failure. Sometimes we fail because we don't give a fuck—not just because we tried hard and it didn't work. We've got to give ourselves a chance to revise by being honest about what we did yesterday. And that's the hardest shit in the world for some reason.

JR: You're often asked about your willingness to be vulnerable, but I'm curious about your willingness to speak well of yourself. Is that something you had to teach yourself or does it come naturally?

KL: I've definitely had to teach myself to do that. When the pandemic hit, I don't think any of us knew what Zoom was going to mean in our lives. A lot of people would ask, "Kiese, can you come do this?" And then I had a lot of friends that asked me to do their book launches. So, once you start doing so much shit on camera, you don't want to fall into the same thought and talk patterns. One thing that's just hard for me is to big up myself. So, to make all of this shit bearable, sometimes I'm like, "All right, I want to boast a little bit. I want to talk about myself in ways that I might not believe, but I want to say it anyway, just to add some spice to the conversation." But that's real hard.

JR: I get it. But it's not that you're boasting, you just speak kindly of yourself.

KL: I've been doing this publicly for eight years, but I've been writing for people's eyes since I was fifteen. I've spent literally two-thirds of my life doing this art. When I was coming up, I didn't see Black people ever talking about themselves in literary form in very generous ways. I saw a lot of rappers do it. And I love them MCs, but I didn't see many people and I still don't. And honestly, whenever I talk about myself kindly, I always regret it. I ain't going to lie to you.

JR: It's a shame how so many of us are raised to not speak well of ourselves.

KL: Some days I just need somebody to say something nice about me, so I need to say it myself.

JR: You are so hopeful. But what are you like when you're alone and not writing? I feel like when we write or teach or speak about writing, something inside us lights up. A more optimistic part of ourselves. Can you sustain that hope when you're not intentionally engaging it?

KL: That's a brilliant question. I'm going to change the word—I think I'm much more faithful off the page than I am on it. Because on it I do want readers to understand that I do have a faith that we can undo this shit. Do we want to? Nope. Can we want to? Yup. But when I'm off the page, I'm very faithful. I believe what people say to me. It's one of my problems. I believe anybody the first time, second time, which means you have to in some way have some sort of faith that people mean what they say, and that people are good. And when I'm on the page, I feel like I owe myself and people more than blind loyalty. But off the page, I believe people until I don't, and when I don't, I don't ever believe, you know.

Kiese Laymon on Revision as Love and Love as Revision

Jordan Kisner / 2022

From the *Thresholds Podcast*, hosted on the Literary Hub website with Jordan Kisner, February 9, 2022. Reprinted with permission.

Jordan Kisner: I wanted to talk to Kiese Laymon because recently he did something that very few writers ever do. He bought back the rights to his first two books from the publisher, revised them significantly, and published them again. One was his novel, *Long Division*, and the other was a collection of essays called, *How to Slowly Kill Yourself and Others in America*. For those of you not proximate to the book world, I can't stress enough how rarely something like this is done. For one thing, you have to pay the publisher to get the rights to your books back. In Kiese's case, he paid $50,000, which is more than ten times how much the publisher paid for them in the first place. Also, most books when they are published are considered done, no more revising, you move on to your next project. Revising your first two books and republishing them is a bold thing to do. Which Kiese did because as he says in our conversation he's developed almost a theology of revision which he says is not just about how you write but also about how you love and how you survive. Laymon is maybe best known for his memoir *Heavy*, which is a memoir about growing up as a Black man in Mississippi, and about his experiences with racism, violence, addiction, and sexual abuse. We touch on some of those topics in this conversation as well so if that's an area of sensitivity for you, take care. Here's Kiese Laymon.

Kiese Laymon: My student Emma Carmichael, who was one of the—I think she was managing editor at *Gawker* asked me if she could run an essay that I had written on my blog. An essay that was called *How to Slowly Kill Yourself and Others in America* and I said, "Sure but you think that there's an audience for that kind of stuff at *Gawker*?" And she was like, "Yes, believe me, trust." And you know that decision to publish with *Gawker*, it just changed my life. I mean, writing that essay changed my life but that essay was on my blog for several months before I put it out to the world. And then when it came out, it went viral and you know if anybody's read *Heavy* you know I spent way too much time in casinos. And I was in a casino, and people kept calling me and I was like trying to lose all my money, I'm like, "Stop it! Trying to fucking gamble and being an addict. Leave me alone!" And everybody was like, "Dude, you got to go to Twitter." I had a Twitter but I didn't fucking like know how to use it. Actually, Imani Perry was the person who called me and was like, "Kiese, you gotta go to Twitter." I was like, "For what?" And she was like, "People are reading you." I was like, "What does that mean?" I think from there my life sort of changed. Obviously, I was doing a lot of writing and a lot of reading before that but that was the first piece that I really put out for mass consumption. And that was the first piece that also went sort of viral. See, this is why I was afraid, 'cause we about to really talk.

JK: I hope so!

KL: I always sort of felt as a writer I was a writer who like, if you put in a small village, I could write shit that the village would think was hot. You know what I'm saying? I could be at the smaller scale, be at a college community, like, you know, like a really small town, maybe a city. I could get enough of the folkways in there and kind of know what pushes and pulls people to where I could write a piece that would get the village talking. But I was not sure that I could expand beyond my village and have people care. The fact that I could write about a small village, where I learned how to write, now that was at Millsaps college, and have it go out to an international sort of audience and have it reverberate, it was very shocking to me. I had a blog but again, when you're blog writing, thankfully, you're writing to a small group of people who sort of know you or know your mama or somebody. So that was the first time I was like, "Okay, so the scale is much bigger, but I can still move the crowd." I knew I could move the crowd on a smaller scale, but that was the first time I was like, "Oh, you can move the crowd on a larger scale." Honestly, I did not think I could do that because at that point I also had gotten 850 something rejections for *Long Division* and everything else I was writing. I kept being told that there is no audience, that there's no larger-scale audience for you. And so when I wrote that essay, and people for whatever reason felt it, and I think felt the rhythm of it, even though they talk about it like that, I think that sort of helped me understand that I could do something I really didn't think I could do. I thought I was at best a local writer who could write really well about local things that local people cared about.

JK: Yeah, it's interesting that you mentioned rhythm, because something that I was thinking about while you were talking is that it must have been a really, like, the trajectory of having something that you wrote to for yourself with kind of the integrity of your own, just like, writing to please yourself in what feels like a sort of smaller stage kind of way, and then having that go really big is the experience of realizing that the way you sound is something that people will listen to rather than trying to break into a bigger [scene]. You know, a lot of people start writing for a *Gawker* or like a New York mag or whatever in some of these bigger venues by pitching and then trying to sound like the venue, trying to sound more like a *Gawker* writer or whatever that might mean. It sounds like that wasn't what that experience was like for you. I'm curious how that experience of sounding like yourself on larger and larger stages, like, did that begin then? What's that journey been like?

KL: Man, that's a great question. Yeah, it's so layered, because I went to Millsaps. I got kicked out of school for taking a library book out of the library. Then I went to Jack State, and then I transferred to Oberlin College, where Calvin Hernton and bell hooks were teaching. I went to that school because Calvin Hernton and bell hooks were there. When I got there, I started really exploring this idea of Black literary imagination that Toni Morrison puts forth. I had been thinking as an undergrad a lot about what it means to write to and for people who don't read and write for a living, right? So how do you actually craft a voice that is particular in a market that is looking for mimetic shit, right? And I was writing about that as an undergrad, and of course, I'm an undergrad, so I'm writing about it all sloppily, and I'm using hip-hop and blues primarily as my text to compare literary stuff to. There was a part of me that just felt like, you know, I taught a lot of hip-hop early on in my career, and Jay-Z had this line in one of his albums where he's like, "I made it so you could say Marcy, and it's all good. I didn't cross over, I brought the suburbs to the hood." Whenever I teach that, I'm always like, "First of all, it's corny, fam. You did not. 'You brought the suburbs to the hood.' Jay-Z is trying to tell his listener who he perceives as a Black young man, 'Look what I did for you. I brought these people to you.'" So I never wanted to be a native informant. Do you know what I mean? Like someone who's like, look, "I'm about to bring you to this part of Mississippi." I just wanted to craft a number of singular voices that were mine, that had integrity, that could resonate with people where I'm from. It just so happens that I was able to create rhythms that people could appreciate who weren't from Mississippi. If it were not for repetition, we wouldn't be on this call today, do you know what I mean? That first essay, I'm doing some things that are sort of interesting but sort of not. But really what I'm doing is I found like three different refrains, and I tried to . . . you know. . . . "How do you make an essay with three different refrains?" It's sort of like antiquated now but like a lyrical essay saying "blah blah blah." I was trying to burst the essay form like for myself privately, on my back, in my room when I was writing that. But while doing that I never thought that it would catch on because you're kind of writing it not to catch on. That's what's so interesting about the question. I don't trust *The New Yorker* audience, I don't trust the *Gawker* audience. I didn't trust the *Sports Illustrated* audience, ESPN audience, I don't know what audiences I did trust. The fact that so many people at first started to feel *that* particular piece—at first it made me wonder what I did wrong. Then of course, as an artist, I was like, "Oh no fam, you just kind of used . . . I mean, you're talking about guns, you're talking about race, you're talking about gender, and you're really doing some stuff with repetition that people hadn't popularly seen done around this topic." That's kind of why people mess with that essay. It's not like the greatest essay in the world, but at the time nobody else was writing publicly about guns, race, gender and space—in that rhythm.

JK: Yeah, I have wondered for a while what it felt like to you as you began to build that bigger and bigger audience, that was full of some people who you really didn't trust, and some people who you were excited to reach. What kinds of pressures felt introduced to you, then? On you or on your writing? Did you struggle with feeling like you needed to change what you were trying to do?

KL: Yes, because you know, like, I'm a teacher and how do you say this? I don't know how else to say it other than you just really want to be taken seriously, yet you doubt that you will be taken seriously by a lot of people. What *Gawker* did after that was they said, "Alright, we're gonna give you a weekly column." They were like, "We want you to do this again, and again, and again." I think the best decision I made at that point in my life—and I wasn't making many good decisions that point in my life was like I was like, "Alright, I don't want to write a weekly column but I want to run a weekly column where I can get other people to write, and I can maybe write once every month, every two months or so." I'm saying that if I were a younger writer and *Gawker* gave me that humongous platform, I would have just flooded. Every week, you would have been reading me. But at that point, I understood there were gazillions of writers out there who were better than me, who didn't have platforms, and I wanted to use the *Gawker* platform to push them. Also, I did not want to continually be expected to write that kind of shit in *Gawker* every single week, it's not sustainable. It wasn't sustainable. I couldn't do it.

JK: Hmm.

KL: But what I could do is I could use that platform to get a lot of folks who I knew and didn't know out into the world. And it worked, like if you look at that stuff that we published on *Gawker*, I mean, there should be like a documentary or movie about *Gawker*, cause that shit, it's absolutely nuts what happened. But also it's just like so many writers who we're reading today in the strange way like got a start right there on *Gawker*. With all of its like, warts and everything else, you know?

JK: Yeah, something that I've admired about your work and your career for a really long time is the way that you've seemed really committed to writing as this coral enterprise, where there are a lot of voices operating together as opposed to just like the one totemic authorial voice. I know you've done that in a lot of different ways from what you did with that *Gawker* column opportunity, to putting in that beautiful essay that's like an exchange between you and Michael Denzel Smith, and a number of other writers. I guess the question I'm trying to ask you is, how does that feel? What's the relationship between your commitment to *that*, to the kind of collectivity of voice in your work and the way that writing is sustainable for you? There's a connection I want to draw between that element of your work and sustainability. Because so much of what you write about is like choosing to keep living, and keep writing, and keep pursuing, and keep sort of pushing towards a better self and a better world.

KL: A lot of it is just that, you know, as a young person, I mean I had a lot of thoughts but like sharing was not one of my, you know, like . . . I always thought that if you had more of anything that somebody else needed or wanted, I couldn't figure out why you wouldn't give it to that person. I remember being in fourth grade and I could have been class president. But instead of voting for myself, I voted for Magic Crum and that vote changed the whole thing and Magic Crum became class president. I voted for Magic Crum instead of me because I knew magic Crum would make a better president. That's not like some like virtuous anything you know, but like, I think that I have that like I believe . . . Imani Perry often says she doesn't believe in cliques, she believes in relationships. Sometimes I want to echo whatever Imani Perry says but I actually do believe in cliques, and I actually do believe in teams, and I want the team to be as wide as possible and I want our teams to share. Especially with something like art, art making, and art production. If I got something, if I got in any door, one I'll never want to be the only Black person in there, I mean, that's just how I am. Whatever I have, I wanna share it. And the multiplicity of voices is just like traditional. I come from a state and a place where multiplicitous voices, voices in the singular individual, and actually like lots of different voices are what make up the blues, the gospel, what people call rock, what people ultimately call funk, that communal kind of like boom, you know, like Jackson, Soul Sonic Boom, it's so communal. Yet, you have to figure out a way to etch out your specific individuality within that boom, and that boom is a collective. We individually don't make booms. Booms are collective booms, and there's an individual sound in that boom that is yours. And like, yeah, I wanna do that. I wanna be. I wanna have a style that people be like, "Oh, that's Kiese." But I also want folks to know that, like, Kiese is connected to a much larger continuum of people out here trying to do good work. That's corny as fuck, but I believe it, which is even cornier, you know what I'm saying? I love a team, you know, and the question is, do you also love an enemy? You know, that's the thing I don't really like to talk about. Teams love to fucking play against somebody, you know? But I love a team. I love being on a team. I love it. The bad thing about that though is like you can get a bad publishing deal, so I'm thinking, "Oh, you know I couldn't get my first book published. You wanna publish me? We're a team now!" Then you're like, "Oh no, you just wanted to make money." You know, we're not a team. Anyway, so yeah. I like team shit and I like collectives. I like to share, and I just want to do that with my art as much as possible.

JK: Yeah, I want to ask you about that publishing deal that you were alluding to in a second. But first I want to ask you just because now I'm curious. Do you love an enemy?

KL: See fam, I do. That's why I shouldn't've opened that up because so much of this book I wrote, *Heavy*, is about my relationship in my life. I've never said it this way, but in my life at different times, it felt like the biggest enemies in my life were my mother, myself, my body, and gambling. Then *Heavy*, in the early iterations of it, I was just like, "I'm coming to get all y'all." But how do you get yourself right? If you are the enemy, what is the like, you know . . . For the first two years of writing *Heavy*, I was writing hard shit that I should have not been writing or taking space before I wrote. Not just to find the jewel or find the memory, but I was doing some of that shit to hurt the enemy, who was me! You know what I'm saying? So, yes, I do love an enemy, fam. But it's a terrible trait to have. It's really terrible to let enemy type shit fuel your art. But I do. I love an enemy. And it's terrible. I wish I did not.

JK: What is that? What does that love feel like? Why do you love an enemy?

KL: Because I love to beat people that think they can't be beaten. You know what I'm saying? See what I'm saying? Like now we're talking. Now, I sound absolutely fucking ridiculous, but the sad thing is, I believe everything I. . . .

JK: You think a lot of people don't also feel that way? I feel like a lot of people feel that way.

KL: I think they do. I think a lot of people feel that way. I just don't think they get on podcasts and talk about it. Honestly, the only way I could beat the casino was to write *Heavy*. The only way I could beat my mom was to write *Heavy*. The only way I could beat myself was to write *Heavy*. Now, that book is doing a whole lot more than all of that, but there's a part of me that needed to see these three different manifestations of things that whooped my ass, that whooped me into the ground, fucked up my relationships with my everything. I was like, "OK, they beat you up. It looks like they're gonna beat you up for the rest of your life. So, like, how can you fight back?" And the only way I knew how to do it was to write *Heavy*. It's so much more complicated than that, but I'm saying on one level, yeah. My mother is not my enemy. I don't wanna—that's why I don't like talking like this, 'cause people reduce it. My mother is not my enemy. But at different times, all of our parents feel like enemies. You know what I'm saying? At least people I know. But the casino don't give a fuck about anybody. It doesn't have a personality. It wants to just continually extract. So how can you beat a casino? You can't unless you write a book about the shit that can make it so you, one, are too embarrassed to go in there, and two, can make up the money that you lost from it. You know what I mean? Like, that's how sometimes my mind works. Never talked about it like that before, but I think that's true.

JK: That makes sense.

KL: [*Laughs*] Okay.

JK: That makes sense, yeah! But what happens when you're like writing a book and part of the thing that you're doing, at least at the beginning, when you're writing a book is about beating an enemy that is also you? How do you write the book where winning is also beating yourself and what's the cost of that?

KL: Yeah, I mean the costs are so extensive. Your body, your sanity, your relationships with reality, your relationships with human beings. Yeah, it costs a lot to write books like that, you know? It just costs a lot to write books like that. If you think that you're gonna be OK no matter what, you just do it. But the thing you also know because you write is that you're not gonna be OK, you're not OK. You know what I mean? Like, you're just not OK, but you can get into this comfortable rhythm of not being OK. Thankfully for *Heavy*, I will say, I want to thank my editor Kathy Belden, and my agent. They saw me write through all these manifestations at different points. They both had to be like, "Homie, slow down, fam. You are going too hard at yourself, and the world does not need to know this." Both of them, to different degrees were like, "Don't do that. Stop doing this to yourself." You know, I'm hardheaded. Sometimes I listened and sometimes I didn't, but I've luckily found—thankfully found—a different writing process for the work I've been working on where I don't have to try to fucking like find a hole in my body and literally pour more fucked up toxic ink into that hole until it, you know what I mean? I don't know. I feel like that shit is cool actually, when you're like twenty-eight. But I was doing this shit at forty-two. It's so not cool at forty-two, fam. It's not the look at that age.

JK: A keyword in your work for a little while now has been revision. You brought back these two books, so you could revise them, but also revision is a pretty big theme in *Long Division*. And you've been writing about revision as this dynamic practice. I'm curious, can you tell me the story of how you started to think of revision in the way you think of it now?

KL: Yeah. I mean, *Long Division* got me to thinking and understanding revision as, not the kernel of potential like radical fairness, but you know, like if not the kernel then one of the kernels of health or my imagined health. *Long Division* helped me think about that as a writing practice. Buying the books back, you know, was yeah. Yes. I wanted the ink, and the paragraphs, and the shape of the books to change but also, I wanted to revisit the process of those books being out in the world because the process of putting those two books out in the world, I don't know if I'm thankful I had that experience. That experience helped make me a tougher person, but it didn't make me a better person. So I wanted to also just revise the experience of putting the books out. *Long Division* particularly to me is about the act of seeing oneself extra textually or texturally and going in and attempting to write oneself in spite of what a master narrator might want from oneself. I feel like it's about a lot of shit, but I think at the end of the day it's about runaway characters being like we want to revise the way that you have written us, and the only way we can do it is sort of to go under the ground together, collectively and and see what we can make. So that's where I started to really think and feel about revision as like a kind of religion or a way of a way of life and a way of loving that makes sense to me.

JK: Yeah. I wanted to ask you about the connection between love and revision because you wrote in that really beautiful essay about your friend, Gunn. . . .

KL: Yeah, Ray Gunn.

JK: Yeah. Yeah. There's this jump between—you say, "Gunn knew he was talking about love and I was beginning to understand this thing about revision." I just wanted to hear you talk more about the connection. That connection goes kind of beautifully elided in the essay. But so, I wanted to ask you in conversation about the way you think about that connection between revision and love.

KL: Yeah. Love is such a scary word for me as a writer because it's the most spectacle laden word that I think we have like, you know, we use it at least in my family, we use it a lot. In my classrooms, people will use it to talk about a paragraph or sentence that they only read once. I remember as a younger writer, I was just like, wait a minute. I claim to love Morrison's Nobel Prize address. I remember when I read it the first time, I'm like, "Man, I love this." Then I was just like, but love necessities like revisitation. How do you love some shit that you don't go back to? I've been in relationships with people who I love. I wanted to see and hear and feel them again. It wasn't like, I love them, and the memory carried, and that was enough. So for me it's just like just the notion of revisitation that is part of love. We love songs, and often we go back and listen, and listen, and listen. Those relistenings give us different portals of entry into us, into a songmaker, into all kinds of stuff. And so like, I just thought one of the basics of love is revisitation, right? And revisitation is part of revision. To revise in love, you have to listen to people outside of yourself. You have to listen to other visions of yourself. You have to mind other people's visions of who you are to them and who they are to you, know what I mean? Plus, I think Baldwin wrote about love and Morrison wrote through love with such tenacity and love, tenderness, and vigor. I just wanted to maybe add something different to it, which is the revision aspect, which is tied to art, and so that's really it. But for me love and revision are just literally like conjoined twins.

JK: I mean that makes sense because much of the way you talk about revision sort of extends past revision as like a writing practice or an art practice into a relational and political and kind of future oriented practice of getting to remake and sort of redeem sometimes or heal things that feel broken.

KL: Yeah.

JK: I think that one of the reasons why people don't do that as openly and as publicly as you do is because it feels scary to be. Then to be putting your emails with your mom whose relationship you're working it through together in these emails, it feels scary to put those emails out to some people in the world. And it feels scary to be saying I was wrong about this or I changed my mind about that. I've wondered for a while if you feel that fear and just decide to do it anyway, or if there's something that supersedes that fear, or if you just don't feel afraid of that.

KL: I definitely feel that fear, for sure. But you know, as I've said in other places though, my duty to the page and to the art kind of overwhelm that fear. Do you know what I'm saying? I feel that fear, but I just don't wanna write wack shit. That's another way to say it. I just don't want to write wack ass shit and it's hard not to write wack ass shit if you're afraid of actually looking at the parts of yourself and people around you that you don't want to look at, and actually looking at the parts that you do want to look at with different or newer sets of eyes. So the hardest thing for me is not to talk about— the scary thing about where I am in my life today is the things that I've done that are terrible in this world, which to me are like hurting people that I purport to love. I'm not afraid to talk and tell anyone in the world about those experiences. I don't want to tell it. I don't want to talk about it publicly because I know that that triggers and harms people, but I'm not afraid to talk about the worst shit I've done in my life. But I *am* afraid to think that I'm doing that kind of work, and then actually not be doing any work at all. It goes back to what you're saying about trying to write like the *Gawker* audience, or trying to write *The New Yorker* piece. I'm afraid, artistically, of being like a hack, much more than I'm afraid of being—or as much as I'm afraid of being a fucked-up person. I want to believe that if I'm doing my best work on the page, I'm doing my best work in life. I want to believe that. I don't know if it's true but I wanna believe it. You know I'm saying? I want to believe.

JK: Something that I've noticed about your work and your writing and other interviews you've given is that you seem to be somebody who thinks a lot about what you want your writing to be doing and how you want it to be sort of in conversation with a literary and artistic tradition. You seem to be a writer who writes and sort of theorizes your writing at the same time. That was another reason why I wanted to talk to you because I feel like you have really clearly defined ideas for the ways in which you want to be pushing yourself forward and trying new things, and also pushing a form forward and trying new things. I'm curious, do you feel like you have to switch between brains? Of like, "This is the thing I want to be doing formally versus the thing I'm saying?" Or "This is my aspiration for my writing versus this is the me that's going to sit down and write?" Or are they the same?

KL: They're not the same. That's what's so interesting to me is I think that there are just different ways to braid essays. You know we talk about braided essays, often, some of it's facetious, but I'm sort of obsessed with that which makes me *feel* a tremendous amount of emotion while it makes me think in a way that might be going oppositional. I love that depth that's created when you encounter that, I do want to create that. I want readers to *feel* their way through my pieces, but I also want them to feel like they are being asked to *think* their way through pieces and make decisions. You know what I mean? Like I don't want to create like spectacle like ever—I mean, that's fucked up to say like, people want to be like, like nobody wants to create spectacle. Of course we want to create spectacle. We want to create some shit that people want to watch. But I also wanna create shit that people wanna watch and like engage with, and think and do something with at the same time, you know? I think that first piece we started talking about was *How to Slowly Kill Yourself and Others in America*, like I was writing about guns and young black people and bullets, and everybody was writing about that. But I think I took people on a narrative, and I used the present at the time that people weren't using a ton of present tense writing. But I think the present sometimes can make people feel more. But then you hit them also with these ideas where they have to think. One of the things I think you have to think about when you're reading some of my shit is like, do I like this motherfucker or not? Like, is this person so whatever that I can ride with them or not? Ultimately, when I wrote *Heavy*, there's the scene when my babysitter, who was twenty-something and I was a young boy, put a breast in my mouth. I was very, very scared that her breasts was gonna smell like whatever food we'd just eaten. When I put that in a piece, it's not to titillate necessarily, but it's also like, not just because it happened. You know? I want readers to be like, "Oh shit. Do I laugh in this scene that is literally like . . . this is sexual abuse. Like, this child is being abused, but that shit is funny, what the child just said." I want that tension to exist. Not the same way in everything I write, but I want it to exist in everything I write. I think that's what the thinking, and the feeling, and the theorizing, and the moving the narrative forward come in. That's what I like. That's what I like to read. So that's sort of what I'd like to try to create.

JK: Yeah. What are you pushing for right now in your writing? What edge are you trying to ride in what you're working on right now?

KL: I'm doing different forms right now, thank goodness. I'm working on film, I'm working on TV. But if we're talking about just literature and prose and stuff, I'm trying to, in this new work, how do I say it? They're ghosts, or what people would call ghosts in my new work. Some of these ghosts are wearing the clothes that my grandmother wore when she was a young person. But those clothes are being attached to a wig head, and that wig head has a wig on it, and the face might be whatever I drew on it. I'm trying to work on people understanding that that is not magic realism. That is not surrealism. That is actually like real, *real*. And so like I'm actually tapping a lot more into sort of like what people call spirit writing now in my new stuff, and it's really scary, but it's where I am and I know I'm writing it cause my granny's about to die. I'm trying to make people think and feel in this new shit, but I'm also just trying to define good and God in like as abundant and particular a way as I can. I haven't ever *really* tried to do that before in my work. Even saying it sounds like, if I were you, I'd be like, "I don't know what the fuck you just said, but OK." You know? But that's what it is. I don't know what the fuck I said either, but that's what I'm trying to do.

JK: I want to talk to you more about spirit writing, but I don't want to take up too much of your time. Do you have spirit? Like in what sense are you playing around with spirit writing? Do you have stuff that you're like reading and thinking about?

KL: I've read Jesmyn, religiously, Jesmyn Ward. In everything I've written, there's always been a scene where there's this character who's wearing what looks like a house gown. And the character, again, doesn't really have a face, but the face is drawn on. I have to take those scenes out of everything I write because they don't—they're too weird and they don't fit. So what I've done is like I've collected those scenes that I've written throughout however long I've been writing, and I've really tried to sit in why. Why was this character the first character in the nightmare that I remember? My first nightmare, this character was hopping toward me. I'm at the end of the driveway, and this character is hopping, and they stick a hole in, like I had a hole in like a shirt. They stick their finger in a hole in my shirt, and when they stick their finger in a hole in my shirt, I knew whatever, like doom, death, something, but that character recurs in real life. Actually, like I believe I've seen or talked to that character. But I didn't feel I had the writing skills to actually like make you believe it, you know? But now I think I do. But the question is scary. It's like, so what happens when you do convince people that this godhead really, like this person, this thing that you call God, which is this sort of like fucking amalgamation of my grandmama's clothes like hanging on a wig head. Like, So what? You know, it's a big so what? But for me it's like I need to tell myself and I actually need to like just make a distinction between what is good and what is God, and what is my grandmama, and what is great, and what is not. I want to do it in ways that you know, like narrative progression and character development, and just sort of like sit in spirit.

JK: I mean trying to define good and God in your writing, that's big.

KL: Yeah, that's what I'm doing in my writing, that's it. I'm trying to define good and God, and create portals of entry for people to come in and redefine them for themselves. I don't know if I'm gonna succeed. Actually, I'm not gonna succeed. But that's what I'm doing. That's what I'm doing.

Bayou Magazine Interview

Marian Kaufman and Nora Seilheimer / 2023

From *Bayou Magazine* online, December 14, 2023. Reprinted with permission.

Interviewer: In *Long Division* the characters' unique voices jump off the page, and the narrative of time travel is both complex and thrilling. Would you talk some about the most difficult and enjoyable aspects of writing this novel?

Kiese Laymon: Thanks for this question. It feels so long ago. The most fun and terrifying parts of writing that book were really sitting in the bodies of those young Black children. I had to sit there and look behind their eyes, feel behind their skin. They're funny kids, but they're tough kids with huge imaginations. So I had to really see what they were hiding, and why they were hiding. That was fun but really scary. They're so young, and so unaccepting, in a way, of death and destruction. They just refuse to believe the world is how it has to be. The books were never meant to be read smashed together. There were three books meant to be read one another after another, so when I was asked to smash them together, it got hard and strange.

I: In your essay "You Are the Second Person," in the collection, *How to Slowly Kill Yourself and Others in America*, you write about the difficult process of publishing your debut novel, *Long Division*. Could you talk about your commitment to the ideas in *Long Division*, and why you refused to compromise its message?

KL: Well, I compromised a lot, but I wouldn't compromise when an editor told me to take the racial politics out of the book. That really was the end for me. I realized the editor didn't respect me or my vision, though I understand why they made such suggestions. I wasn't going to write a book based in Mississippi about black children being written off the face of the earth with no racial politics. That would be like writing a book based in the forests of Montana with no trees. It's a cool concept, but it's bullshit. With all these other books being written with little to no racial politics, I couldn't figure out why I'd imitate one of the biggest failures of American literature.

I: In *How to Slowly Kill Yourself and Others in America*, you used actual letters, emails, and eulogies from your real-life relatives and friends, messages originally intended for a small audience. Will you talk about the process of putting those voices into a larger, cohesive work?

KL: That's a great question. I wanted my book of essays to come out first, and I wanted it to be filled with voices. Kanye's *The College Dropout* was really an inspiration because of all the voices he uses in that text to create one piece of seamless work. I wanted to do that with my first book. Aunt Sue's pieces came as one huge letter. I broke it up. Kai, Mychal, Darnell, Marlon, and I wrote letters to each other, too. I also think all humans are made up of a ton of voices, and I wanted to get a lot of my own voices in the piece.

I: What audiences did you consider while writing your essay collection, *How to Slowly Kill Yourself and Others in America*? How did thinking of these different audiences influence the final product? How do you continue to consider audience while writing?

KL: I wrote to the people or characters who are actually in the book. Sometimes some of those characters are on the front row. Other times, they're in the balcony. White men never got the front row of any of those pieces. That was necessary if I wanted to tell the truth and tell the truth how I wanted the truth to sound.

When I think of audience, I think of who I most want to respond to a piece. That person or group of people is the audience for me. In the Uncle Jimmy [essay], I most wanted to hear him respond. In the essay, "How to Slowly Kill Yourself and Others," I most wanted to hear how all those murdered Black kids would respond. Often, like in my new work, I flip up audiences within a piece, too. That's a lot harder, I think.

I: You have two books forthcoming from Scribner, a memoir, *Heavy*, and a novel, *And So On*. How do they converse with your previous work? Are you exploring any new territories in content or style?

KL: Yeah, they are really new. *Heavy* is the hardest thing I've ever written in style, context, expectation, genre, everything. It's a memoir, but it's a whole lot more. That book scares me. It's scary to write about what's been done to your body, but scarier to write about what your body has done to make others vulnerable. *And So On* owes a lot to *Long Division* for what it taught me. It's far less ambitious in form, but far more ambitious in terms of character and subtext.

Sitting in Silence: Special AWP Edition Interview with Kiese

Maurice Carlos Ruffin / 2024

From *Sitting in Silence* Substack, February 6, 2024. Reprinted with permission.

Maurice Carlos Ruffin: What are your earliest memories of reading or writing stories?

Kiese Laymon: I've never been asked that. I remember drawing a lot as a kid and writing sentences in the clouds of those drawings. My mama made me write all the time, but I don't remember actually writing much of that stuff. I remember writing in the clouds in third grade.

MCR: Every once and a while on social media, we get to see one of the legends' early selves. Like Octavia Butler bucking herself up in her notebook. Can you talk about what you were trying to do in some of your earliest writings? I mean before amazing work like *Heavy* and the essay collection and *Long Division*. I think writers would be curious to know what your before work was like. So what were you doing and how did you buck yourself up?

KL: That's a great question. I was amped when I say Ms. Butler hyping herself up. I wrote essays in my student paper in high school in 11th grade. I wrote a lot of rhymes before that. But when my friends gave me props for something I wrote and I won these two Mississippi Scholastic Press awards, I was hooked.

Then I wrote a lot of essays in college. Editing a lot. Wrote and directed plays. All in college. Didn't really write fiction until grad school. Then that's all I wrote for about seven years. Then I used my understanding of scene and sensory details to bolster my nonfiction. That's why I'm here. What did you write before you really wrote wrote!?

MCR: Bruh, I'm not sure I'm really writing yet. But way way back? When I was a high school senior, I wrote a monthly piece for a magazine called *Sitting on the Stoop*. It was just two young dudes talking about school and dating. That lasted like two issues lol. In college and after, I fiddled with short stories. Mostly imitations of Jhumpa Lahiri, Stephen King, and John Kennedy Toole. Then I wrote comic strips in law school out of boredom and a little music for my bass and guitar. It wasn't until I went back to what my teachers gave us in high school (Maya Angelo, Anne Moody, the Harlem Renaissance writers, etc.) that I started to figure out some things. There's so much wisdom the ancestors provide. I think you have to grow up to really feel it in your chest. Who do you look to when you're trying to get to that place? Who speaks to you?

KL: I definitely feel that. And the comic strips meant a lot to me too. I always come back to Morrison and Baldwin. Mostly specific books. Honestly, I read you and Deesha and Robert and Jesmyn to get right. Y'all's talent humbles me. And then because I know and love y'all, I feel I gotta get to work. And I'm just starting to accept that most of the work is experiencing earth and humans and senses. But I also lean a lot on oddity. Weirdness.

MCR: Weirdness is underrated. I taught *Song of Solomon* last year for the first time and was shocked to really understand how strange it was for Milkman to wander through a whole jungle in America only to run up on an old mansion with an apparent witch named Circe living in it. Like Circe from ancient Greek poetry, Circe. She was just chilling and waiting on him to show up. That's the kind of weird people don't talk about. You know what's not weird? Your use of language. I feel like a lot of us out here have learned a lot from your work. One thing that struck me is how you present our voice in your work. Too often I hear from new writers from the communities being pushed by editors into using "mainstream" or "accessible" voices. But mainstream or accessible isn't really a thing. How do you decide what you want your page to sound like?

KL: That's an incredible question. Mainstream and accessible are definitely imaginary. I want most of my pages to be polyphonic but also decidedly Black and Southern and original. I think it's so hard to make a page bend to our voices. It's so so hard. You do it incredibly well. But even in *Heavy*, I framed the book with *bend* and *been*. That's an ode to how they're the same sound in the place that raised me. What do you think of so much of work being called "voice-driven" by critics? I'm often like, what narratives aren't driven by a voice. It might be a boring voice or a clichéd voice. But all of our work has a voice that can drive a narrative. I just want the voices to be familiar and weirdly innovative.

MCR: I think that some people look for a way to downrate people who don't come from the same background as them. So if you're Black, Southern, queer, or whatever, that isn't seen as work. That is seen as adjective work. As in they put a qualifier on it to let you know they won't fully respect it. I think it was Min Jin Lee said one of her college professors told her she needed to learn how to write normal, but she correctly assessed that he needed to learn how to read her and the rest of the world. There's more on earth than is dreamt of in Shakespeare and Phillip Roth. And I like those dudes, but rappers can tell stories and so can the lady who sells suppers at my church. Speaking of being good, every time I turn around you helping someone. Just now you're backing up Lit 16. I've witnessed you working with young people in my hometown. I know you supporting this organization and that organization. What does it mean to you to help us like this and do you have any thoughts about good ways for the rest of us to help?

KL: You got me going on all the dynamic storytellers in our spaces! As far as what we can do, we can ask folks how we can be of service with our talent. That's the most important thing. And if you have good hometraining, you must use it most brilliantly in our community of writers. You share. You don't abuse anyone. You try hard as you can to keep your word. And, I'm learning now, you take big breaks when possible and you lovingly say "I'm sorry but I can't" sometimes. What do you think our writing communities need most in 2023?

MCR: Good question. I'm a history lover. I like learning about earlier generations of writers like the Harlem Renaissance or even, as I'm learning now, the poets and playwrights who were writing in the Mediterranean from like 600 BC through the time of Christ. If someone told us that people might be reading our work in a hundred years or a thousand years, I think that might help us all have more perspective and not be so anxious about our triumphs or failures. I consider myself a role player. If my job is to focus on providing a view of my community in New Orleans before the big waters come, then so be it. On the other hand, I like that line from Drake where he raps that he "drinks to his accomplishments" with friends. People know and I mentioned in the introduction to this interview some of the many things you've achieved. Can you mention a small thing you did in celebration of winning the MacArthur? I think it's important for all of us to take those moments to breakdance, dunk the football on the goal post, or sing with joy. Even if you sing flat like me.

KL: Mannnn, folks need to know how long it took me to answer this question. I'm thinking about the role player comment. I feel that deeply. I like that. Same for me. Maurice, I haven't really celebrated yet. I mean, I took the semester off. But that was to get medical stuff done. I got my mama and aunties and friends some gifts that they really wanted. If I was still in Oxford, I would have gotten some season tix to the Grizzlies.

MCR: You've given us so much, so I'll be lovingly pugnacious and say don't be afraid to give yourself something too! Speaking of giving, one of my favorite concepts you wrote about in *Heavy* (a certified banger) is Black abundance, which is the opposite of a meager mindset. I think about that literally all the time. I have to stop myself from naming everything I write, Black abundance, because that's what I think so many of us are working toward. When you talk to younger people about this concept, what do you tell them? What does it mean for you, them, and the future?

KL: You know what's wild, Maurice? When I read *American Daughters*, I felt that Black abundance. The characters in that book aren't simply good or virtuous or perfect or responsible. They are committed and flawed. They are courageous and afraid. They are excessive and reserved. So yeah, when I'm talking with young people, I ask them what do they love most about being Black and young. That answer, no matter what, is that Black abundance. It's not nearly as rigid as Black excellence. It's not utopic. It's not dystopic. If anything, it's heterotopic. And that's sorta where all my work is headed. What you think of abundance in *The American Daughters*?

MCR: Thank you for the blurb, by the way! For sure, heterotopic is the word. I'm going to save that one for future use hahaha I want to present a version of us we haven't quite seen. The good bad ugly but mostly the loving.

Food for Thought:
An Interview with Kiese Laymon

Constance Bailey / 2024

Personal interview conducted August 2024.

For context, Kiese and I were originally scheduled to sit down and chat with Dr. Regina Bradley during a visit to Georgia State University in February 2024 for the Center for Studies on Africa and Its Diaspora (CSAD)'s annual Read-a-thon, but the visit had to be rescheduled. Given our demanding schedules and the passing of Kiese's grandmother, it became increasingly difficult for us to sit down and talk, or chop it up, in the parlance of folks our age who are from the South. Instead, we decided to augment our conversation through email. Rather than provide a list of disjointed questions and answers, you'll notice italics in many of my questions. These are insertions that I have made to impose organization onto the interview and replicate a conversation. It is a conversation albeit a written one. The main difference here is that had this been a verbal exchange, the italics would be much longer because I am extremely long-winded as is Kiese, but his responses have not been altered here in any way. To maintain the fidelity to the conversational nature of this exchange, it's written in the vernacular because this is how I'd converse with a Black GenXer from Mississippi. What can I say, if you know, you know. Mississippi we in hea!

Constance Bailey: Between *Heavy* and your recent essay about Jr. Food Mart that opens Kate Medley's photojournalistic book about gas stations in the South, I would almost describe your relationship with food as a love/hate relationship, but that feels reductive. How would you describe your past or current relationship with food?

Kiese Laymon: Tough question. I'd like to say I love food, or I love to eat. I don't love food or really love to eat now. There are a few places in Mississippi that make me really happy to eat but right now I'm in one of those places where I really don't like the idea of eating honestly. I'm working on it.

CB: I definitely understand that. I too have a complicated relationship with food. While we're on the subject of food, you've recently started at least one food justice initiative connected to food in Mississippi if I'm not mistaken. Can you elaborate on that initiative? How it came to be and how people can support? What other Mississippi initiatives have you initiated or are on the horizon?

KL: Oh yes indeed. It's just the most incredible thing I've had a chance to be a part of. Last two summers we brought about twenty-five kids from Mississippi to JSU. And led by the Margaret Walker Center, the kids learn about the origin of the food they eat while learning about creative writing for a week. And they get a stipend. It's our attempt at love.

CB: That's beautiful. I'm going to be a hater and say that it should've been at Alcorn State, but in all honestly, I love the folks in the JSU English Department. I can't say enough wonderful things about them. In thinking about students and writing, I often think autobiographical work makes for great writing. I often envision teaching a Mississippi memoirs course where I would teach *Heavy, Men We Reaped, Memorial Drive, Coming of Age in Mississippi*, and maybe even *Black Boy*, though it might technically be an autobiography, I'm not entirely sure. At any rate, what are your favorite memoirs (you can only pick five) and what unifying element, if any, exists among these?

KL: Geesh. *Men We Reaped. Fire Next Time. Black Boy. Caged Bird.* Machado's *Dream House*. They all are as strong on the line as they are conceptually.

CB: Oh okay, I've never read Machado's *Dream House*. I'll definitely add it to the top of my To Be Read pile. I saw that you recently shared a couple of stories that my friend Addie Citchens wrote for *The New Yorker*, and I was so excited, but this is not anything new. You often platform other creatives, especially those from our home state and the South, and although the answer seems self-evident to me, can you talk about why you do it?

KL: I mean, I wouldn't know how not to share whatever juice or platform I have with our folk. That is the only reason we are here. Share what you have a die. And Addie is just a bona fide contender for illest writer alive right now. Folks are about to find out if they don't know.

CB: I'm really sad to say that I haven't read enough of Addie's writing and we've been down like four flats since we did a biomedical research internship at Ole Miss when we were in high school. The irony isn't lost on me that neither of do anything remotely connected to that. I can't wait to catch up on her stuff after I submit this manuscript, lol. Speaking of friends, my friend Richelle Joe is a huge fan of your work, and she told me that she's curious about the power or value of writers exploring where they're from. This resonated when she was reading *Heavy*, with Hanif Abdurraqib's new book, and S. A. Cosby's books, among others. It feels special when an author writes about, from, and for "home." Can you discuss this a little?

KL: Constance, honestly, my Grandmama died a few weeks ago and I realized I've been writing from her and calling it Mississippi. Her body gone. A big part of home is gone. A lot of my hometraining is gone. And I'm scared of what this all means for my art and my heart.

CB: Yes, I saw that. I think we were going to work on some things for this project, but I wanted to honor your time with her memory and with your family of course. There are very few figures as central to my praxis as my grandma, so I understand completely. In thinking about grandma's, I often include quotes or proverbial expressions from my grandma in my titles, where do you get your ideas for titles?

KL: You know we come from folks who love dual meanings. All my titles have at least three distinctly different meanings. Some are more obvious. Some aren't. *Heavy*, for example, is all folks have written about as a title. But it was also my feeling myself in that specific book, and saying Heavy is the head of the joker who wrote this book, because line for line, I wrote the mess out of that book.

CB: Yeah you did. I'm super excited about the podcast that you just dropped with fellow creative writer Deesha Philyaw. Can you talk a little bit about how the project came to be, and what other projects are happening in the near future that you're excited about?

KL: Honestly, I've been heartsick since the pandemic, and Deesha had this idea that we could talk to our favorite writers as a way to work through the blues. I forgot it was all being recorded. We were just trying to love on folks who love on us with their work.

CB: On your podcast you and Deesha talked about writing about your parents. In their stories and a lot of others I've heard the difficulty is writing about a strained or broken relationship with a parent who harmed them. Do you have thoughts about writing about parents from a different place, such as loss or longing? How might that be different?

KL: I love the question about writing about parents from a different place. I was trying in *Heavy* to show that longing. That connection with your parent if it's just y'all growing up is absolutely sublime. Wherever you situate yourself to write about parents, I just hope folks do it with style and different registers.

CB: Changing gears just a little bit, who is your favorite Mississippi emcee?

KL: My favorite Mississippi emcee is KRIT, He got me through some cold, cold days up north.

CB: Yeah, KRIT is great. I'd love to interview him for a project on Gulf South music. KRIT always makes me think about growing up in Mississippi so I'm excited about the children's book but I'm wondering why now? Was this something you always wanted to do?

KL: I wanted to make books for kids before I wanted to make books for adults. During 2020, I just started thinking about Black kids and softness and some of the games we played outside in Mississippi. So I built a book around the idea of a kid from New York coming to Mississippi. It's a new take because we usually talk about kids coming down from the midwest. It's a soft beautiful book.

CB: That's what's up. So my last question is actually connected to the question is also about upcoming projects. What's the status of *Good God*? You reference it in several interviews, but a children's book is next. Did you table it for a future date or is it source material for a script, screenplay, etc.?

KL: *Good God* should be out next fall. *City Summer, Country Summer* is coming in April.

CB: I'm excited. I can't wait to read both. Thanks so much for taking the time to answer my questions.

Index

Abdurraqib, Hanif, 132
Absalom, Absalom! (Faulkner), 20
abuse, 17, 32, 38, 41, 44, 57, 63, 112, 122, 128
activism, 10, 108
addiction, xi, 17, 26, 30, 32, 112
Adichie, Chimamanda Ngozi, 10, 40
Adjei-Brenyah, Nana Kwame, 60
African writing, 8
afro, 75, 84
Afro Futurism, 5
Afro Surrealism, 5
Alcorn State University, 131
Alexander, Margaret Walker, xii, xv, 6, 131
All about Love (hooks), 28
American Daughters (Ruffin), 129
André 3000, 5–6
Angelo, Maya, 127

Bailey, Constance, 130–33
Baize (character), 11, 36, 39, 44, 61, 108
Baldwin, James, 6, 10, 15, 17, 19, 21–22, 28, 38, 108, 120, 127
Bambara, Toni Cade, 6, 15
basketball, xii, 33, 54, 65, 71
Beatty, Paul, 33
Beloved (Morrison), 61
Bereola, Abigail, 24–29
Black Boy (Wright), 20, 131
Black children, 6, 18, 125, 133; boys, xii, 3, 12, 26–27, 31, 39, 41–42, 59; girls, 26, 41–44, 61
Black Lives Matter, 85, 90
Black writers, x–xi, 5, 8, 20

Blanche on the Lam (Neely), xivn1
Braxton, Charlie, 6
Brinkley, Jamel, 28
Broom, Sarah, 60
Brothers Writing to Live Crew, 6
Brown, Meghan, 34–43
Butler, Octavia, 6, 126

candor. *See* Laymon, Kiese: honesty
Catherine Coleman Literary Arts and Justice Initiative, xii, xv, 102
Citchens, Addie, xiii, 131
City (character), 3–5, 8, 10–11, 15, 36, 37, 38, 39, 103, 104, 105, 106, 108, 109, 133
civil rights, 22, 73, 82–83
Color Purple, The (Walker), 60
Coming of Age in Mississippi (Moody), 131
coming-of-age novels, 9
Cosby, S. A., 132
COVID-19, 73, 82, 85, 95, 97–98, 105, 110, 132

Dunbar, Eve, 6

eating disorders, 32, 57
Ellison, Ralph, 37
Evidence of Things Not Seen (Frederick), 11

Faulkner, William, 20
Fire Next Time, The (Baldwin), 21, 131
fraternity, 65, 70, 84–85, 95
Frederick, Rhonda, 11

135

freedom fighters, 63
Freedom Rider, 106
Friday Black (Adjei-Brenyah), 60

Gabriel, Jacob, 9
gambling, 11, 22, 32, 117
Gawker, 112–16, 121
Gay, Roxane, 3–7, 9, 11
Giovanni, Nikki, 10, 21
Giovanni's Room (Baldwin), 21
Go Down, Moses (Faulkner), 20
Good Man Is Hard to Find, A (O'Connor), 20

Hamer, Fannie Lou, 84
hampton, dream, 6
Heads of the Colored People (Thompson-Spires), 33, 60
hooks, bell, 28
Hsu, Hua, 6
Hurricane Katrina, 3–38, 61

I Know Why the Caged Bird Sings (Angelou), 131
In the Dream House (Machado), 131
Invisible Man (Ellison), 37, 43

Jackson State University, iv, xii, 98
Jay-Z, 114
Jim Crow, 38, 68
Johnson, Kenneth, II, 11–14
Jones, Tayari, 28
Joseph, Marc Bamuthi, 27

Kaufman, Marian, 124–25
King, Martin Luther, Jr., 31
King, Stephen, 127
Kisner, Jordan, 112–23

Lahiri, Jhumpa, 127
LaVander (character), 3, 36–37
Laymon, Kiese: on art, xii, 11, 13, 16, 18–19, 21, 23–24, 27, 32, 53, 57–58, 60–61, 97, 100–102, 110, 115–16, 117, 120–21, 132; arthritis, 107; on Barack Obama, 31–32, 40–41; on Black children, 4, 18, 124; Black Southerness, 127; Black women, 11, 14–15, 27, 35, 102; community, ix–x, 4–7, 38, 41, 46, 49–50, 101, 108, 113, 128; critics, 127; on Donald Trump, 29, 31, 53–54, 105–6; essays, 10, 18, 27, 34–35, 42, 53, 74, 97, 112, 121, 125–26; ethics, 61–62, 74; family, ix, xi, xii, xiii, 13–14, 17–18, 21–22, 25, 28, 31–32, 38–40, 44, 98, 100, 106, 120, 132; father, 19, 31, 45–46, 106; food, xii–xiii, 22, 25, 28, 122, 130–31; geography, xii, 7, 43; on George Bush, 105; giving back, 10; God, 12, 61, 68, 70–71, 83, 89, 91, 94, 98, 101, 123, 133; grandmama, 18, 20–21, 29, 97–102, 104, 123, 132; healing, 97; history, 7; home, 6, 8, 17, 20–21, 27, 29, 31, 38, 63, 73, 75, 84, 87, 99, 101, 131, 132; honesty, ix, xii, 7, 22, 24, 53; humor, xii, xiii, 17, 23; imagination, 4, 9, 15, 19, 26, 39, 102, 114; laughter, 23, 103–4, 122; love, xiii, 3, 5–7, 9–12, 14, 17–20, 22–23, 28–31, 33–34, 36–37, 39, 41–42, 46–48, 50, 57–59, 63, 74, 76–77, 86, 95, 97–98, 100–106, 108, 110, 112, 117, 119–21, 127, 129–33; MacArthur Foundation Grant, 128; masculinity, 58–59, 63, 106; memoir, 11, 14–15, 17, 19, 21, 24–25, 42, 52–53, 57, 96, 112, 125, 131; memory, 6, 14–15, 21, 23, 53, 117, 120, 132; mom, 15, 18–19, 22, 25–27, 30–31, 35, 42–43, 53, 59–60, 99, 118; narrative, 48, 122–24, 127; patriotism, 14, 63; poetry, 53, 60, 127; policing, 22, 27, 31, 48, 49, 70, 86; politics, xii, 10, 40, 74,

94, 124; poverty, ix, 7, 10, 42, 48, 99; privilege, 10, 41; publishing, 4, 6, 9, 97, 117, 124; queerness, 32, 128; race, 4, 7, 11–12, 28, 41, 43, 46, 71, 79, 103, 107, 115; racism, 10, 12–13, 17, 19, 71, 103, 112; reading, 9, 15, 20, 25–26, 30, 39, 43, 52–53, 60–61, 74, 81, 92, 102, 113, 115–16, 122–23, 126, 128, 132; revision, 5, 7, 15, 52, 97, 112, 119, 120; sexuality, 7, 41, 107; sports, 58–59, 115; stories, 5, 13, 19, 39, 41, 53, 56, 59, 78, 106, 127–28, 131–32; storytelling, 5, 128; the South, 3, 6, 13–14, 20, 24, 38–39, 70, 99, 109, 130–31; transformation, 6; voice, xii, 6, 11, 35–36, 87, 89, 93, 114, 116, 127; vulnerability, 19, 58–59; on war crimes, 105; weight, 13, 15, 21, 25, 35, 56, 66, 78; white supremacy, 5, 58, 104; writing stories, 126

Works: *And So On*, 125; *City Summer, Country Summer*, 5, 15, 133; *Good God*, 5; *Heavy: An American Memoir*, 5, 11; "Hip Hop Stole My Southern Black Boy," 41; *How to Slowly Kill Yourself and Others*, 3, 5, 7, 11, 15, 17, 18, 34, 35, 36, 40, 42, 53, 97, 100; *Long Division*, 3, 5, 7–11, 15, 17, 18, 36–39, 41–44, 53, 61, 104, 105, 112, 113, 119, 124–26; "My Vassar College Faculty ID Makes Everything OK," 9

Left of Black (Neal), 10
Lorde, Audre, 10
Lott, Eric, 37
Love and Theft (Lott), 37
Lumumba, Chokwe, 45–50, 51n1

Margaret Walker Center, 12, 131
Memorial Drive (Trethewey), 131
Men We Reaped (Ward), 131

Midnight in Chernobyl (Higginbotham), 60
Millsaps College, 74, 84, 113–14
minstrelsy, 37
Mississippi, x, xiii, xv, 6, 8, 13, 17, 20, 24–26, 40, 47, 56, 58–59, 61, 63–66, 68, 70–78, 80, 82, 84–92, 94–95, 100, 102, 103–6, 108–9, 112, 114, 124, 126, 130–33; Forest, 100; Free Press, 65; Jackson, 13, 20, 45–51, 64, 73, 82, 86, 88, 90, 98, 117; Mississippians, 63, 75, 77–78, 81, 91, 95, 106; Natchez, 10; Pass Christian, 10; state flag, 63–65, 72, 75, 78–83, 85, 86, 89, 90–92, 94, 95
MMA, 9
Moody, Anne, 127
Morrison, Toni, 28, 35, 106, 108, 114, 120, 127
music and musicians: André 3000, 5–6; *Aquemini*, 5; *ATLiens*, 5; blues, 34, 114, 117, 132; *The College Dropout*, 125; form, 34; funk, 117; gospel, 35–36, 117; Halona King, 12, 36; "Hate on Me," 12; hip-hop, 6, 12, 27, 36, 41–42, 114; hip-hop journalism, 6, 112, 124–25; "How I Got Over," 12; jazz, 33; Jigga (*see* Jay-Z); Jill Scott, 12; Kanye West, 35, 125; KRIT, 133; Mahalia Jackson, 12, 36; Maxwell, 36; mixtape, 12; "Monster in the Night," 12, 36; *My Beautiful Dark Twisted Fantasy*, 35; Outkast, 12; "Ova da Wudz," 12; "Pretty Wings," 36; "Public Service Announcement," 12; rappers, 110, 128; rock, 117; *Stankonia*, 5; Tupac Shakur, 35

National Book Award, 28, 53, 60, 64
Neal, Mark Anthony, 10

New Yorker, The, 115, 121, 131
Noor, Poppy, 31–33
NPR, 9

Oberlin College, 114
O'Connor, Flannery, 20
Okri, Ben, 8, 9

Pejic, April, 97–101
Perry, Imani, 6, 113, 116
Peters, Scott, 52–62
Philyaw, Deesha, xii, xv, 127, 132
prison, 38, 84, 106

Radiolab/WNYC Studios, 63–96
Ratcliffe, Jane, 103–11
Reckon True Stories, xv
Renaissance, Harlem, 127–28
Roth, Phillip, 128
Ruffin, Maurice Carlos, 126–29

Salvage the Bones (Ward), 38
Sanchez, Sonia, 10
Seilheimer, Nora, 124–25
Smith, Bessie, 35, 38
social media, xii, 69, 126
Song of Solomon (Morrison), 127
surrealism, 122

Thomas, Monet Patrice, 17–23
Thompson-Spires, Nafissa, 28, 33, 60
Tretheway, Natasha, xii

University of Mississippi, 17, 20, 65–66, 70–72, 102

Vassar College, 9, 40
violence, 21–23, 25–26, 28, 30–32, 41, 112

Walker, Alice, ix
Ward, Jesmyn, 6, 9, 20, 38, 61, 123
Welty, Eudora, 19–20

What Doesn't Kill You Makes You Blacker (Young), 60
White Boy Shuffle (Beatty), 33
Williams, Serena, 28
Words Become Flesh (Joseph), 27

Yellow House, The (Broom), 60
Young, Damon, 60

About the Editor

Photo courtesy of the editor

Constance Bailey is an assistant professor of African American Literature and Folklore at Georgia State University. Her research focuses on Black women's comedy and humor, Black speculative fiction, and African American folklore/oral traditions. She is coeditor of *Get It While It's Hot: Gas Station and Convenience Food in the U.S. South*, which is forthcoming from LSU Press in spring 2026.